MELANIE SANDERS STEWART, PHD

BUTTERFLY
on the Highway

A Guide to Experiencing Spiritual Transformation in the Face of Adversity

Copyright Notice

Butterfly on the Highway
A Guide to Experiencing Spiritual Transformation in the Face of Adversity
Melanie Sanders Stewart, PhD

© 2018, Melanie Sanders Stewart

Published by Anointed Fire House
Cover Design by Anointed Fire
www.anointedfirehouse.com

Author photograph by Tracy Rowell at Reflection Images
www.reflectionimages.com

ISBN-13: 978-0-9993380-4-9
ISBN-10: 0-9993380-4-8

Disclaimer
This book contains material protected under International and Federal Copyright Laws and Treaties. Any unauthorized reprint or use of this material is prohibited. No part of this book may be reproduced or transmitted in any form or by any means, electronic or mechanical, including photocopying, recording, or by any information

storage and retrieval system without express written permission from the author/publisher.

The author and publisher have made every effort to ensure that the information in this book was correct at press time. The author and publisher do not assume and at this moment disclaim any liability to any party for any loss, damage, or disruption caused by errors or omissions, whether such errors or omissions result from negligence, accident, or any other cause.

I have tried to recreate events, locales and conversations from my memories of them. In order to maintain their anonymity in some instances I have changed the names of individuals and places, I may have changed some identifying characteristics and details such as physical properties, occupations and places of residence.

Dedication

To the Almighty God of the Universe for pursuing me with your ever-lasting love.

To Jesus for hearing the cry of my heart and answering it.

To the Holy Spirit for inspiring me to write just as you inspired the authors of the Bible.

To my mom, Frances, and my sister, Patrice, for always lending me an ear or a shoulder and loving me through it all.

To my daughter, Alyx, for being my tireless cheerleader.

Acknowledgments

Sharon Benson—you always told me the truth, though it was sometimes hard to hear. You never neglected to love me unconditionally, and that made it all worthwhile.

Janice Kay Gunter—you always make me feel like I can do everything! You are a great teacher and an even greater friend. Thanks for cleaning up my grammatical errors in the first draft. Love you, Big Sis!

Tiffany Buckner—your Spirit of Excellence shines through all you do. Thanks for being such a wonderful editor and publisher. You made me feel like I could really complete this!

My fellow Media Specialists in my district—because you always strive for excellence at work and have such loving support for one another, I just want to brag about how your care helped me to press forward with my dream.

Russ McLeod—for identifying the depths of my visions in vitro and encouraging me to birth them out.

Table of Contents

Introduction XI

Chapter 1 ....
The Darkest Hour of the Soul 1

Chapter 2 ....
I Don't Deserve This 17

Chapter 3 ....
The Heart of the Matter 37

Chapter 4 ....
Out of the Deep 59

Chapter 5 ....
My Personal Apocalypse 77

Chapter 6 ....
The Formula 91

Chapter 7 ....
Going Where You Don't Want to Go and
Doing What You Don't Want to Do 97

Chapter 8 ....
Things are Not What They Seem to Be
....109

Chapter 9 ....
You Don't Have to Do Life Alone................115

Chapter 10 ....
Beauty for Ashes................................141

Chapter 11 ....
The Struggle......................................155

Chapter 12 ....
Get Out..163

Chapter 13 ....
The End of the Journey (Or Is It?)
....177

Introduction

Butterfly on the Highway is a compilation of the journeys we undertake as we progress through life. It is a story of stories--a saga of sagas. Sometimes, we have a choice of which road in life to take, but sometimes, like a butterfly on a busy highway, we are tossed about, and a path is chosen for us. We wake up one day to find ourselves suddenly in the line of fire, traveling down a road we would not have chosen, and we question ourselves. We handicap and stunt our growth by thinking if we'd turned right, turned left, or stood still perhaps none of it would have happened. We would be in a better place physically, spiritually and financially ... a place where we would live and thrive in a state of unmatched euphoria. To dwell on this and overwhelm ourselves searching for immediate answers is counterproductive and a moot point. Life is not a state of perfection, but rather, a slow, painstaking process that blows us from one direction to another like a butterfly on a windy day. We question our identities and how we've ended up in the realities we've been subjected to--only to wish that we were someone else. The fact of the matter is…you are who you are right now, and there is a greater purpose behind it all. Sooner or later, we all see the light at the end of the tunnel, whether it be through life or death. We reach a plateau where all travels and questions come to an end, and then, we are ready for the next step. This is where the real journey begins.

Chapter 1

The Darkest Hour of the Soul

"Have you heard anything yet?" Maggie asked.

John glanced from the road briefly to give her a confused look.

"Heard what? From who?" he asked, perplexed.

"From God."

John released a deep sigh and gripped the steering wheel tighter.

"No. Nothing yet."

They rode on in silence for a while, each of them deep in thought. Finally, Maggie couldn't stand to replay the day over in her mind anymore. She needed some distraction. She reached over and turned on the radio. The song "I Trust You" by James Fortune was playing. The lyrics seemed to describe all they felt after spending the whole of the

Chapter 1: The Darkest Hour of the Soul

day at the hospital. The prognosis was not good. The doctor flung around terms that were more than a little difficult to comprehend, but there were a few words they understood all too easily—"Take care of all your business while you can."

A storm was brewing on the horizon. Ominous, dark clouds quickly rolled in, almost covering the sun completely. There was no hope left, and both John and Maggie were drained at the thought that this time next year, she would not be there at all. What about the girls? They needed a mother. What about her family? She'd always been the dependable one — the glue that held everyone together. What about John? She was his life — his reason for living. What would he do now? None of this had been in the plan. They were supposed to grow old together. That's how it should be. She'd just celebrated her birthday a month prior to the news, and it was disheartening to know that it was probably her last.

The song continued. As the singers' voices

Chapter 1: The Darkest Hour of the Soul

began to swell with impassioned certainty, something moved deep within Maggie, and she began to cry. There was so much to do before her heart gave out. Yet, one thought kept moving to the forefront of her mind— the question that had plagued her since her first heart palpitation years ago: "Would everything be alright?"

"Your job performance for the past few months has been subpar. Therefore, the board has reached a consensus. Andrew, you are terminated from your position effective immediately. Security will escort you to your office to retrieve your things and then to your car." With a wave of the hand, Andrew was dismissed from a job he'd dedicated the majority of his days and nights to. He thought of all the years he had neglected family events and his own personal health in order to make sure all his work was done and to make sure that the bosses and investors were satisfied. As he walked down the hallway, Andrew felt like his life was over. "How

Chapter 1: The Darkest Hour of the Soul

will I pay my bills? What will everyone think? How could they do this to me after all the time I've committed to working for them and all the things I gave up for them? What will happen to my family? Why now? Why me?"

Melinda was five months pregnant when she found out about the affair. Oh, he was a sneaky one, all right. He made every effort to cover up every move he'd made between her and the "other one." Yet, even though he did all he could to keep her from finding out—and it did work for a long time—Melinda found the letter from "her" in the armrest of his truck. Her suspicions were finally confirmed, even though she could do nothing about the affair.

All throughout her marriage, Melinda had been verbally abused and controlled by her husband. He moved her far away from her family and wouldn't allow her to have any friends.

Chapter 1: The Darkest Hour of the Soul

Anytime she talked on the phone, he would snatch it out of her hand to see who she was talking to. He wouldn't even allow her to have a cell phone, saying it would give her easy access to all the men he believed she would mess around with if he weren't as careful as he was. He was so paranoid that he would go outside and rake the dirt driveway everyday so he could tell if any other cars came into the yard.

He came and went as he chose, especially after she became pregnant. Melinda first became suspicious when he would come in and head straight to the bathroom before he greeted her. He stayed in the bathroom for a while—always on his cell phone. Whenever she asked to use his phone for any reason, he would scream at her, telling her to stay away from his stuff. After this, he would pocket his phone before she could even see it.

One day, he got careless and left the phone on the kitchen table when he walked outside to speak with a neighbor. Melinda quickly searched

Chapter 1: The Darkest Hour of the Soul

through his texts, discovering steamy messages from some girl named Dawn. After she read through them, the destination of his nightly outings became clear.

Melinda decided to step totally into the fray and call Dawn. When she answered, Melinda asked her who she was and why had she been sexting her husband. She also asked her if she realized that he was a married man with a baby on the way.

No sooner than her last question left her mouth, her husband walked in. She quickly regretted picking up the phone. He grabbed the phone from her ear, threw it across the room, and began slapping and dragging her across the floor. After he was done, he stormed out of the house, leaving her passed out in a wretched and sobbing heap on the floor all night long.

The next morning, as Melinda nursed her throbbing head and bruised skin, fervently praying that the baby was okay, he stormed into the house in

Chapter 1: The Darkest Hour of the Soul

a rage, overturning tables, chairs, and whatever stood in his way. When he finally reached her, he grabbed her battered shoulders, shook her and demanded to know who had been at the house last night. There were tire tracks all over his raked yard. She screamed that she didn't know—she had been unconscious until just moments earlier. Maybe someone turned around in the yard, but no one had come to the house that she was aware of. He did not believe her, so he started once again to pummel her body to "teach her" that he was the "wrong one to be messin' around on." Melinda prayed for someone — anyone — to come and rescue her.

"Hey, Dionne. I just want to check and see if now is a good time to connect?"

"It sure is! I've been waiting to speak with you for a while."

"Well, good. So, tell me how was your weekend? How are you doing today?"

"I'm feeling okay right now, but I've had

Chapter 1: The Darkest Hour of the Soul

some times of depression, and I feel a little out of sorts right now. I just want to know what's going on behind the scenes. Are they really getting what they deserve? Are they experiencing karma or am I the only one who's miserable?

      Dionne spent a good half-hour going over all the feelings that had been rolling around in her stomach since the break-up. Jealousy. Fear. Vengeance. Hatred. She had never before had such intense emotions, and the turmoil of everything she was feeling was draining her. The betrayal. The lies. The resulting argument and the dismantling of friendship were almost too much for her to bear. And where was God in all this? Whose side was He on anyway? Surely, He had to be on her side—she had done everything right. She was dedicated, loyal, and truthful. Yet, it seemed as if she was the one suffering greatly while the perpetrators of her heartbreak waltzed away seemingly oblivious of the destruction they'd left in their wake. Where was God? Did He even care? If He was truly a loving Father, wouldn't He bring swift justice and make

Chapter 1: The Darkest Hour of the Soul

them pay? Were they weeping silently? Would they go down to the pits of the same hell she had been through and be tormented forever for their sins? How was God, whom she'd always referred to as "The Great Equalizer," going to work this out for her good? Was He even fazed by this, or were her cries going unnoticed?

All these torturous questions played over and over in Dionne's head as she sat quietly in her dark bedroom. This had become her custom of late- retreating into her darkened sanctuary after a day of trying to piece her life together and pretend everything was okay.

It was in her sanctuary one night when Dionne's head was about to explode with the ruminations of what happened and the mystery of if they would pay or not that she sought out a psychic connection. She wanted someone who could find out what exactly was going on behind the veil and what would occur in the future. Never before had Dionne even considered delving into the arena of

Chapter 1: The Darkest Hour of the Soul

the paranormal because she'd always believed that such connections were not of God. But she was desperate. So what if it was another source that provided the insights?! God wasn't talking anyway! In the back of her mind, Dionne thought about how disconnected God was from her life, and she really wanted a connection with someone — anyone — who could help her figure this out! After all, God wasn't trying to save her. Somehow, she would have to save herself — by any means necessary.

My Story

Many times, it's easier to take the advice of someone you know who has undergone the same things as yourself. It is difficult to relate to someone's pain if you have never experienced the pain of like manner on your own.

In the past, I've had people come to me, sharing their complaints and worries. Honestly, I had no inkling of an idea as to what they were feeling, so my empathy level was surface level, at

Chapter 1: The Darkest Hour of the Soul

the most.

Yet, there have been folks who have stepped onto my path who seemed to have sung the same sad songs that I have sung. That's when my heart tends to tremble and tears well up in my eyes. I fully understand the soul-crushing, world-flipping experiences they are facing. I understand what it's like to be going confidently down one road when an unexpected detour turns you completely around and delays your journey. All of this happens while you deal with whatever debris is littering your path, almost like that of the aftermath of a hurricane.

Plan B is never as attractive as the first plan. Plan B is always unintentional. It is what you do if your first plan fails. Of course, you never want the first plan to fall apart because it's the plan where you have everything under control, and all the desires of your heart are met. Your children will be well-behaved geniuses who contribute life-changing innovations to society before the age of thirteen. Your house will be immaculate and the envy of

Chapter 1: The Darkest Hour of the Soul

every HGTV viewer. You move so quickly up the career ladder that you'd almost declare you were on a turbo-speed escalator ride up to the well-appointed, glass-ensconced corner office of CEO.

Then, all of a sudden, you're in a tail-spin, knocked senseless by some tragedy that takes you by surprise. All your well-laid plans suddenly disappear in a cloud of smoke, and you're left grasping at gray wefts of dust dissipating into the air.

If you've ever been brokenhearted, you know you can actually feel the pain throbbing in your chest. I was there. Crumbling and shattered to my very core. "It happened…again," I thought…
"How could this have happened?"
"I don't believe it."
"I hate my life."

Tears of despair and agony flowed from my eyes in waves. It was like someone died —and in a way, this was true — the deepest part of me died

Chapter 1: The Darkest Hour of the Soul

that day. The death of a relationship that seemed full of promise and hope is never an easy thing. Add to this the confusion and uncertainty of where things will go from here makes the situation all the more frightening.

I didn't know what to do. I just sunk deeper and deeper into misery. I spiraled at full spend to rock bottom, but all was not lost. You see, the choices I made on that journey inspired me to write this book. It was during this time of my life, when I was most confused and disoriented, that I panicked and made choices that were influenced by desperation, ignorance, and doubt. That point in my life yielded some of the darkest hours I had ever experienced.

My life became a murky mess that I could not navigate through with any glimmer of confidence. I wallowed in bouts of self-pity and Satan was my constant companion within these depths. The enemy of my soul most likely stood as close as an arm's throw from me, salivating and

Chapter 1: The Darkest Hour of the Soul

rubbing his hands together with glee as he quickly realized that this was indeed the most opportune time for him to capture my soul and claim it as his own. He told me lie upon lie about myself and about God, and I believed everything he said.

In my desperation, I spoke to anyone with ears who gave me an ounce of attention. I talked about my heartbreak and asked repeatedly why someone as nice or as good as I was could be going through the hell I was going through. I was full of conceit and self-adoration. As a matter of fact, "why me" was my mantra.

I found myself needing validation--constantly--and I had so many things going through my mind that I felt I had to give them the space to speak. A part of me was searching—searching for a word or a simple phrase that would set everything right in my world.

I needed someone who understood my anguish — someone to help me sort through the

Chapter 1: The Darkest Hour of the Soul

wreckage that was now my life, and try to salvage whatever fragmented pieces of my heart that we could find. After all, I seemed too paralyzed to do it on my own.

It took the jarring words of a truthful and very no-nonsense friend to impact me with the force of a slap to the face and awaken me from my stupor. This helped me to finally face my reality. I'll tell you some of the things she said later on in the book, but know that what she shared cast a harsh light on my mindset up to that point and revealed the true condition of the only relationship that really mattered — my relationship with God. That revelation was just what I needed to start me on a journey of discovering the truth of who I really am, who I am to become, and to who I belong to.

> *You intended to harm me, but God intended it for good to accomplish what is now being done, the saving of many lives. (Genesis 50:20).*

The points you will uncover while reading

Chapter 1: The Darkest Hour of the Soul

this book are lessons that I learned during the most difficult times in my life. I'm sharing these lessons with you in hopes of making your journey a little straighter than the haphazard path I traveled.

Though I cannot guarantee you a Sunday afternoon stroll down Easy Street, I can assure you that your mind will become awakened to every possibility to live the best life you can if you only adhere to every word in this book. You will experience progress. So, commit yourself to hope, healing, discovering who you truly are and to (finally) celebrating a life of wholeness and freedom. Let's roll!

Chapter 2
I Don't Deserve This

David left Gath and escaped to the cave of Adullam. When his brothers and his father's household heard about it, they went down to him there. ² All those who were in distress or in debt or discontented gathered around him, and he became their commander. About four hundred men were with him. (1 Samuel 22:1, 2)

There is something strange about life — I mean more strange than the usual. You can be sitting there, minding your own business when something sneaks up on you and sends your life spiraling down a path you never intended to go down. It doesn't matter who you are, how much influence you may have, or where you have been.

Chapter 2: I Don't Deserve This

All that matters is you are alive, and you must experience life, whether you want to or not.

Sometimes, life takes a turn for the better; sometimes, it takes a turn for the worse. But one thing is sure —life often changes without our agreeing to the change in the first place. We are sideswiped with situations and circumstances that throw us off balance, and the reality is we don't know where to go, what to do, or which way to turn. We are full of confusion, and we definitely don't like that feeling. Before the winds of change blow in, we are steady in whatever course we are on at the moment. We are working at our normal nine-to-five jobs, going to our prospective homes, getting a little nutrition and relaxation, and beginning the process over again the next day. Or we are entertaining the prospects of committing to a long-term relationship because the time seems right. Or we are about to set our sights and seventy-two months of payments on a beauty of a new ride that will turn the heads of our co-workers and our frienemies.

Chapter 2: I Don't Deserve This

Boy! Do we have it good or what?! We're in the zone and ready to go. Our lives are pregnant with hopes and possibilities. All of a sudden and out of nowhere, comes a reality so ruthless that it shakes us to our very core! It just happens. With no warning, no slowing down, and no end in sight. During my teens, I watched movies on a show called "The Graveyard Shift." These were thrillers or horror stories that were advertised to not be "for the faint of heart." Usually, the backstory of the movie started off simply enough. Boy meets girl. The unsuspecting family moves into a new neighborhood. Someone goes for a walk. And all of a sudden, some terrifying creature comes into the picture and wreaks havoc on the innocent souls who you have grown to know and love from the time the movie began.

Well, that creature may have suddenly appeared for the person on the screen, but the audience knew all along that something was about to happen. This is because of the eerie music that played in the background. For me, the hair on my

Chapter 2: I Don't Deserve This

neck would stand straight up, and I would sit with mouth agape in wonderment that the actors could not feel instinctively what I was feeling while sitting on the sofa. I would try to project my warnings to them by yelling at the screen or by positioning myself around the sofa where it would be safest for them to hide if they were with me. Yet, to no avail, the characters in the stories did not sense the terribleness that was about to happen and moved unwittingly towards the monster in the closet.

Unfortunately, life has no soundtracks and no background music set to warn us that our routines are about to change — that life is about to take an unexpected detour down Mystery Lane, and our plans will begin to crumble at our feet.

You didn't plan to lose your job after twenty years of loyalty to the company you started working for right after college. You didn't plan to get a divorce from your high school sweetheart. You didn't plan on having chronic pain so excruciating that you just want to end it all.

This change wipes you out and leaves you sitting, rocking back and forth, wondering when the hammer's going to stop falling. You become debilitated, depressed, and hopeless. Things are out of your control, and you don't know when or if things will get back to normal. Or worse —things change so drastically that you have to learn to adjust to a new normal. And things never return to the way you planned.

How Did I Get Here?

1 Samuel 22:1, 2 gives us a snapshot of the life of David. The Golden Boy of Israel was on the run for his very life. King Saul was constantly lathered up in a jealous rage against this giant killer. David had become Israel's darling, replacing Saul in the hearts of the people. And Saul knew his reign was fast coming to a close. Yet, he would not go down without a fight. A king bowing to a shepherd boy — preposterous!

Chapter 2: I Don't Deserve This

Saul devised a plan to extinguish the glowing flame of David's popularity by attempting to assassinate him. Instead of being the darling of the court and held in high esteem by the people of the city, David suddenly became a fugitive.

Can you imagine the horror the newly-anointed King of Israel faced while fleeing for his life and moving from town to town like a nomad? David planned to remain in the palace serving Saul until God's appointed time for his reign to begin. He was perfectly content with playing his harp and seeing to the king's needs, after all, Saul was God's first anointed.

It was never part of David's plan, or even his demeanor, to carry out a coup to dispose of the mighty king and usurp his authority. For David, whatever way God saw fit to consign him to the throne was up to God because He chose David in the first place, and David trusted God implicitly.

David knew full well that to "wait on the

Chapter 2: I Don't Deserve This

Lord" would give him a secure and stable beginning to his reign. He wasn't rushing into anything, and he respected Saul as being covered by God.

Yet, none of this mattered to Saul. Every time he looked at David, it was as if thirty devils jumped on him. In fact, the word does say that an evil spirit came upon Saul and he tried to drive a spear into David a couple of times as he played the harp.

So, there David was, hiding in a cave. Assisted by a rag-tag army of folks who were either in debt, discouraged or just plain tired of the conditions of their lives. I'm sure there were many times that David wondered, "How in the world did I get here — from wandering the palace to wandering with the dregs of society? What happened to the promises? What about the prophecies?"

And there are people right now who wonder the same things.

- "This is not how my life was supposed to

- turn out."
- "How did I get cancer? I'm vegetarian. I'm the healthiest person I know. What happened?"
- "How did my debt get so bad that I can't afford to eat and pay bills?"
- "How can I survive another beating like this?"

Let's face it — if you look into the lives of random strangers, you would be surprised at some of the anguish they may be experiencing. The questions they have about where life is taking them play through their minds like a song on loop.

David, also, was in anguish about his situation, and expresses that anguish in Psalms 55:15—

Listen to my prayer, O God, do not ignore my plea; hear me and answer me. My thoughts trouble me and I am distraught because of what my enemy is saying, because of the threats of the wicked;
for they bring down suffering on me and as-

Chapter 2: I Don't Deserve This

sail me in their anger. My heart is in anguish within me; the terrors of death have fallen on me. Fear and trembling have beset me; horror has overwhelmed me.

The turmoil which David felt would have overwhelmed many people today, even to the point where they would likely remove themselves from the situation permanently. Yet, David persevered and cried out to God with an impassioned plea to shelter him until the disaster passed (Psalm 57:4). God did intervene on his behalf with many blessings and evidence of His grace as Saul pursued David for what some theologians believe may have been ten years. God was with David every step of the way. David's story proves that though He may not come during a greatly wished-upon timetable, God definitely is in the thick of it with us, and His graces appear right on time. David certainly bore witness to the verse *"greater is He that is in me, than he that is in the world."* (1 John 4:4) David stood his ground and petitioned the Lord to show up for him. All the same, we should continue to endure until we see the salvation of the Lord. Too many give up the fight just before God brings a breakthrough. No matter what Satan throws your way, stand your ground and trust that the salvation of the Lord is on its way.

What to Do When it All Hits the Fan

There are three things you should do whenever mayhem enters your life, leaving you dazed and confused. They are:

1. Understand who you really are.
2. Take everything directly to God.
3. Praise and worship God despite how your situation may currently look.

Understand Who You Really Are

And the Lord shall make thee the head, and not the tail; and thou shalt be above only, and thou shalt not be beneath; if that thou hearken unto the commandments of the Lord thy God, which I command thee this day, to observe and to do them.

Chapter 2: I Don't Deserve This

(Deuteronomy 28:13)

Above is just one of the thousands of promises our Father has made for those who belong to Him. All the resources of Heaven lay at our disposal due to the price that Jesus paid for us at Calvary. The love of God is an everlasting love (Jeremiah 31:3) that is available to each of us way before our first appearing on Earth (Psalm 139:13; Jeremiah 1:5). He longs to shelter you (Psalm 46:1-6), hold you in His arms (Isaiah 41:10), and stand with you against your most formidable enemy (2 Thessalonians 3:3). During the times of your life when your greatest moments of faith collide with the fears which threaten to overpower you, you can trust that God is there, ready to keep you from dangers seen and unseen.

As a joint heir with Christ (Romans 8:17), we automatically have all the advantages afforded us through His blood-bought sacrifice. We are victorious; we should believe this and behave as highly-favored children. In one of his poems,

Chapter 2: I Don't Deserve This

thirteenth century Persian poet, Rumi, insists that life is rigged in our favor, but Paul's declaration speaks closer to my heart when he states, "And we know that all things work together for good to them that love God, to them who are the called according to his purpose." (Romans 8:28).

It is God who keeps predators at bay. He keeps your children from being led astray. He softens the hearts of authority figures on your behalf. He brings the right people across your path. And He thwarts the attacks of the enemy. As a child of God, you need to remember that you have nothing to fear. You can be audacious in your faith because you know that over three thousand promises in the Bible speak directly to what God is willing to do on your behalf. After all, Numbers 23:19 (NIV) states, *"God is not human, that he should lie, not a human being, that he should change his mind. Does he speak and then not act? Does he promise and not fulfill?"* He is true to His word. You don't need to be afraid of the devil or whatever struggles and heartaches may come your

Chapter 2: I Don't Deserve This

way. God has equipped you with all the forces of Heaven to stand alongside you — fighting every adversity that comes your way, so whenever the devil comes with his sinister provocations, you can respond with all the force of Heaven!

Who ARE You?

Like me, you may need a heavy review of who God says you are to Him. Many times, the truth of our positions get lost in the lies that the world and the enemy keep pummeling us with. Oftentimes, our self-image gets a bruising because of the constant torment from those who are set against us. For this reason, we need to make a conscientious effort to remind ourselves of who we actually are. Take some time every day to read God's word and speak truth over yourself and your loved ones. As you say these things aloud to yourself, you strike back at the lies that have embedded themselves as core beliefs in your heart.

The time I speak about who I am is usually on my way to work. I have an hour drive, so I use that time to pray and speak words of life over myself. I have also recorded myself speaking the scriptures that reflect my position as a child of God, and I listen to them as I am going to sleep. You see, I need to solidify within myself and with unwavering confidence that God is for me. No lie of the devil can stand against that level of assurance. Below are some of the scriptures which speak to who we are and the benefits that the Kingdom of God provides for us — benefits that we have because of His love for us and the great sacrifice of His Son, Jesus, at Calvary on our behalf. Create a habit to speak life over yourself starting right now.

1. **Who You Are**
- You are the head and not the tail; above and not beneath (Deuteronomy 28:3).
- You are a royal priesthood; a chosen generation (1 Peter 2:9).
- You are a joint heir with Christ (Romans 8:17).
- The same power that resurrected Jesus lives inside you (Romans 8:11).

Chapter 2: I Don't Deserve This

- You are a child of God (Galatians 3:26).
- You are transformed by the renewing of your mind (Romans 12:2).
- You are more than a conqueror (Romans 8:37).
- Blessings overtake you (Deuteronomy 28:2).
- You are a temple of the Holy Spirit (1 Corinthians 6:19).
- By His stripes, you are healed (1 Peter 2:24).
- You can do all things through Christ (Philippians 4:13).
- You are the light of the world (Matthew 5:14).
- You are loved by God (Ephesians 2:4)
- You are fearfully and wonderfully made (Psalms 139:14).
- No weapon formed against you shall prosper (Isaiah 54:17).
- You are set high above all nations (Deuteronomy 28:1).
- You are blessed with every spiritual blessing (Ephesians 1:3).
- You are the salt of the Earth (Matthew 5:13).

- You are God's masterpiece (Ephesians 2:10).
- You are forgiven (1 John 1:9).

Take Everything Directly to God

God is concerned about every aspect of your life. He *"perfects that which concerns you"* (Psalms 138:8 KJV), meaning that whatever is on your mind is also on His mind. God is in control of the whole universe, and He controls everything that goes on in our world. He wants you to come to Him with absolutely everything. We tend to seek after the things of the world that we passionately want; if we would only seek after God with as much enthusiasm, everything would fall into place (Matthew 6:33).

We must pray fervently — with all the power and passion we can muster. And we must be consistent in our prayers. Most people, after they see their prayers have not been answered, develop a diminishing prayer life — they don't pray with any hope that their prayers will be answered. They lose

Chapter 2: I Don't Deserve This

heart, which allows the enemy to implant doubt and unbelief, which will, in turn, further delay the answers they were originally seeking. As humans, when we truly desire something, we go after it with our whole heart. The same goes for prayer. We tend to pray according to the intensity of our desires. If we really desire something to happen, we keep pressing forward in prayer about it.

Dr. Iris Delgado, the author of **Satan, You Can't Have My Miracle** (2012), asserts that "action and obedience to God's Word will keep you on the cutting edge of the miraculous. Father God will do the impossible for us according to the things that are going on inside of our hearts and the things that occupy our minds. Our prayer life prepares us for all the assignments for the day" (p. 74).[1] To experience the miraculous workings of God in our lives, we must begin to pray with such great zeal and passion that our fervency opens up the way for God to perform majestically in our lives.

Chapter 2: I Don't Deserve This

Praise Him In Spite of How It Looks

Psalms 57 shows that in spite of his exile deep in the caves surrounding his homeland, David still relied on God and praised Him. David looked at his situation, remembered how God had blessed him in the past, recalled the promises of his anointing, and praised God for how He was working in his life. We too have to sing praises and give blessings to God, even when we don't understand what's going on. Our confusion is no excuse for our refusal to take action. We must say to God, "I'm going to praise you no matter how this all works out." Our faith dictates our praise, and our praise validates our faith. We believe He is for us, and even if things don't turn out the way we want them to, we know **that we know THAT WE KNOW** that He is working everything out for our good. Sometimes, we need to exalt the name of the Lord before things start moving. Psalm 50:23 says it this way; "*Those who sacrifice thank offerings honor me, and to the blameless I will show my salvation* (NAS)." So, no matter what is going on in your life or how it may look, praise God for what He has done in the past

Chapter 2: I Don't Deserve This

for you and praise Him for how He is going to show off for you with whatever is on your heart.

As you learn the importance of who you are, open up fully to God and praise Him in every circumstance; your faith will increase, and your moral fabric will become transformed as you praise Him. You will be able to identify the unlimited power which is accessible to you and recognize the moments that God's Spirit moves on your behalf. Determine right now to embed the above principles within your life, and you will soon witness a life transformed beyond anything you would ever dream!

Notes

1. *Delgado, I. (2012). Satan, You Can't Have My Miracle. Florida: Charisma House.*

Chapter 3

The Heart of the Matter

All too often, we see things that look good, but they are not really of worth. I used to pride myself on knowing a good thing when I saw it. Anytime I thought that something was perfect or wonderful, I would sink my teeth into it and give it my full effort and I would nurture whatever that thing was. I committed to it totally, and I put a lot of effort into it. In other words, I know gold when I see it…or so I thought.

I blatantly ignored all the red flags I got from the relationship, which included his criticism about the simplest things, his ability to disappear without my knowing his whereabouts and his intense mood swings. I was thrown off and uncertain,

Chapter 3: The Heart of the Matter

but I thought that all I had to do was keep working hard and giving it my all. You see, I really wanted the relationship to work, and I was willing to do whatever it took to stay within a certain "comfort zone." Hey, after all, I had companionship, someone to go out with and someone to treat me like a lady. At that time, all that was very valuable to me.

I did not consult the Lord about anything except for very surface things. My heart finally had what it longed for — someone to take care of it. I thought it all was ordained and blessed by God because, of course, I'd been patient, the timing was right from my perspective, and (most importantly) I was ready.

I have always believed the old adage "God helps those who help themselves." I felt I needed to do everything in my power to attain the joy and love I was seeking. I think part of me did not trust the Lord with looking out for my best interests; after all, there were many disappointing relationships

Chapter 3: The Heart of the Matter

in my past. At the same time, God did not seem to be in any hurry to rectify the situation and connect me with my "dream man." I had to take matters into my own hands. God had a whole world of turmoil to take care of so surely, I could handle a relationship that appeared to have been dropped into my lap by Him. I moved forward without paying attention to the warning signs, and I tried to skate through without prayer.

It kind of reminds me of Sarah. She and Abraham had a direct promise from God, and the promise was that they would parent a great nation. Yet, there she was — a wizened old lady well past her child-bearing years and childless. Well, Sarah became impatient and took things into her own hands. She told Abraham to take her handmaid, Hagar, and impregnate her so that they could jump-start the promise with a child of some kind. When the little bundle of joy was on the way, the tingle of anticipation was short-lived. Sarah grew jealous of Hagar. When the baby arrived, the unrest that ensued assured there would be no peace in the

Chapter 3: The Heart of the Matter

home. You know the story — the result of Sarah's impatience was far-reaching as it became the catalyst for the intense unrest now experienced in the Middle East.

If Sarah had waited for the promises of God to come full circle, everything would have been fine. How much like Sarah are we? We wait for the right job to come, and that opportunity seems like it is taking forever. We wait to get the right connections, but they never happen. We wait for that special someone, but that person never appears. And, as our clocks, biological or personal (goal-wise), keep ticking away, we become anxious as the enemy whispers in our ears "It'll never happen. God's not thinking about you." For this reason, we try to make things happen on our own. That's when things go awry.

> *"But those who wait upon God get*
> *fresh strength,*
> *They spread their wings and soar*
> *like eagles,*
> *They run and don't get tired,*

Chapter 3: The Heart of the Matter

They walk and don't lag behind."
(Isaiah 40:31 MSG)

It's often said that God works in mysterious ways. And though we may be perplexed about our situations, the timing, the heartbreak, and the uncertainty about what will happen next, we must believe that God has allowed things to happen to transport us from one phase of our lives into another.

I don't like change. I like for things to stay pretty much the same as long as they are comfortable. Change is disruptive — it puts me in a state of discomfort and inconvenience. I become easily irritated and stubborn if demands are placed on me to make a sudden change — especially when I have developed a system that works for me.
"If it ain't broke, don't fix it," I always say. Yet, inevitably something forces me to move. I'm shoved into unfamiliar territory, and I begin to panic: "What's going on? Why is this happening now? Oh, no! Help!"

Chapter 3: The Heart of the Matter

In spite of all my pleas to remain static and unchanging, I am forced to move out of my comfort zone into a place where I must trust my boss, acquaintance, or whoever initiated the change in the first place. This is a scary place to be. It's an unknown world where the tides can change at the unpredictable whims of a disconnected entity—someone who may or may not have your best interest at heart.

Trials and disappointments are the same way. They force you to move out of your comfort zone. No matter how much you may plea and resist, change is coming, and nothing but the hand of God can stop it. As the Bible says, *"God's ways are not our ways. His thoughts are not our thoughts"* (Isaiah 55:8). No one can be certain of why problems may be surfacing at a specific point in time, but we are given the task to trust God and allow Him to work through His agenda and position us as He sees fit. If we resist, God will sit back and allow us to have our temper tantrums, and after we

Chapter 3: The Heart of the Matter

are spent, He will continue with His plan to move us along.

Now, I can't tell you why things are happening in such a way, at such a time, and many people have sighed, "Lord knows it's been so long!" All I can tell you is that His word says we will not be given more than we can bear. Yeah, I must say that sometimes it seems that God thinks we can bear the weight of the world like we're Atlas or some sort of cosmic superhero, but we must remember He is all-wise and He is not against us. He knows our limits and will cause the trial to cease at just the right time.

Crash and Burn

Okay. Let's be real for a minute. When it comes to heartbreak brought on by an ended relationship, we've got to admit to ourselves that from the get-go, we knew that what we were beholding was not pure gold. What we got a hold of was a little pyrite, or what is more commonly known as "fool's gold." Back during the 1800s, when Cali-

Chapter 3: The Heart of the Matter

fornia experienced its renowned Gold Rush, it was common for miners to mistake this mineral for real gold. After all, it glistened like gold, it had similar coloring, and it gave the impression that it was the real thing. Many times, miners who found this counterfeit gold would hide their discoveries, sell everything they had to buy equipment to extract their finds or purchase the land surrounding their finds. They'd spend an exorbitant amount of time gathering their new "riches." When they had a sufficient enough hoard, they would pack it up on their mules and ride to the nearest bank or assessor's office. Can you imagine the immense disappointment they experienced once they found out their newfound wealth was little more than dry, brittle rocks and totally worthless? Many a miner went to an early grave after crashing and burning, losing everything in an attempt to have it all.

Well, the same thing happens to us. We find people who possess most or all of the qualities we think we're looking for — they have good jobs, don't live with their mothers and treat us with some

Chapter 3: The Heart of the Matter

semblance of respect. We invest all we have — time, nurturing, our listening ears, and yes, our bodies in order to procure this "gem." We think we have finally arrived, only to find that we have totally disappeared from our true selves in an attempt to make sure our lovers aren't going anywhere. Let's say that he's a guy, for example. Later on, we come to find out that he's not all he was cracked up to be. He's not as financially wise as we first thought. He has more baggage than LAX during the holidays. His hygiene leaves much to be desired. His impeccable manners have dissipated. His connection to the God that he initially claimed he loved with all his heart is pretty much non-existent. And now, we're at a loss, wondering what happened and what to do. We can't believe that we were so duped to consume ourselves with this counterfeit, and now, we feel so lost, hurt, and confused.

Glitter Instead of Diamonds

I remember my pastor's wife telling me (after I told her about this fine brother pursuing me)

Chapter 3: The Heart of the Matter

some years ago, "That's just the devil. He knows you're vulnerable right now because you're seeking a relationship, and you're ripe for the picking. This guy is not for you. He doesn't have a heart for God."

Of course, the hairs on the back of my neck stood up, and I got that sista-girl attitude, thinking, "Who is she talking about? She doesn't know my man! We talk about God every day, and he loves Him." So me, in my blind foolishness, allowed myself to be courted and charmed by one of the worse cads in human history. Move over, Casanova! This guy knew exactly what tactics to use to get whatever flavor of girl fit his mood at the moment. And, since I tend to come off as what some call a "Miss Goody Two Shoes," all he had to do was go to his bag of disguises and find the mask labeled "man of God."

This man was a man who I was just beginning to trust wholeheartedly. (Mind you, I said "just beginning." Luckily, he had some ways to go

Chapter 3: The Heart of the Matter

before I got in too deep). He soon lost patience with a woman he deemed as "difficult" and left the car while it was just getting up to speed! He grew tired of paying lip service to a God he wanted no dealings with, and thankfully, left before I totally embraced him.

My wisdom, much like Elvis, had temporarily left the building, and I ignored the warnings from my pastor's wife and the gut feeling I had deep inside myself. I didn't want to hear anything contrary to what I wanted to hear. I wanted a fulfilling relationship and jumped on the first thing smoking, blinded by the "glitter" of his outer covering.

Because of our longings, we tend to ignore the guidance of the Spirit when we are in situations like this. We want something so bad that we believe we deserve it. We've been all we can be, treated people nicely, and gone to church diligently. We've worked hard, healed the sick, gone above and beyond the call of duty. We need something because we're not getting any younger and the pool of

Chapter 3: The Heart of the Matter

available singles is starting to look shallow. What's a good woman to do? Wait forever? After this, we proceed to insert a human being into our lives who has no longing for us, other than what he or she can get from us for the moment. We don't include God in this equation because we don't want to hear what He has to say. Maybe God just wants you to be friends with the guy so that you can witness and guide him to Christ. Maybe He just wants you to be acquaintances. Whatever. You don't want to hear it, so you fawn and preen over someone who has no intention of committing to you at all.

Though we get all the signs, have the feeling that what we see is just gold-plating, we hurry up and invest in this venture, only to crash and burn when we find out our "precious" was actually worthless.

It's Complicated

I listened intently as Matt told me of the constant pain he was suffering. No, it was no longer something physical that stopped him from

Chapter 3: The Heart of the Matter

moving forward. The surgery to repair the hernia was quite successful. Now it wasn't his body that spasmed with terrible pain — now it was his heart.

Matt spoke about how Candy had seemed to move on past their marriage and the victimizer had become the victor. She, in spite of her infidelity, was thriving and reclining in the arms of the one who'd instigated the affair, with a new baby to carry on the legacy of the new family.

They were seemingly happy, and yet, there Matt was just barely hanging on to his sanity. Though he was faithful to the very end of their marriage, Matt felt ashamed of how things seemed to be turning out. There he was, a man in his forties, living in the family home, working at the same job, not going anywhere and he had no perceivable prospects.

He felt condemned by those around him. The "poor Matt" stares and whispers haunted him

Chapter 3: The Heart of the Matter

every time he entered a family function or church alone. He felt so forlorn. Nothing had turned out the way he thought it would. Where was the justice? Where was his reward for doing right? Why was he the one constantly plagued by guilt and condemnation?

When I asked him what all this lamenting was costing him, he simply replied, "Everything." He couldn't seem to move forward. His only escape from the constant memories and feelings of inadequacy in his life was at work, but his joy there was short-lived because it had become so routine. After work, he found himself clinging to new vices to find some distraction or relief from the pain. Yet, giving in to this momentary "pleasure" only invoked feelings of anxiety as to when the hammer would fall, and he would pay greatly for his sins. He was miserable — a prisoner of self-pity and constant self-deprecation.

Chapter 3: The Heart of the Matter

Pressing Forward

Perhaps, you are dealing with a constant reflection on something that occurred in your life that you just can't seem to get over. Whether it is something someone did to you or something you willingly participated in, the resulting feelings are the same — violation, regret, humiliation, inadequacy.

I have found that through the situation, whatever it may have been in my life that occurred in one area, the tendency was for the catastrophic nature of it to tumble over into other areas of my life, such as my career, finances and my relationships with others. And because of this, the situation would become magnified so greatly that I would be left in a ball of agony. There were times when I thought I would never truly smile again or experience a wholehearted laugh. Joy and happiness were totally depleted from my life. What could I do when all I wanted to do was crawl into a dark corner somewhere and wither away? I was ready to give up, but I learned some special lessons from the

Chapter 3: The Heart of the Matter

Apostle Paul that helped me move forward and regain ground.

In the Bible, Paul forever presses forward in spite of things going badly. He was falsely accused, arrested, imprisoned for extended amounts of time, shipwrecked, and bitten by a serpent, among other discomforting and distressing events. Fascinatingly, Paul seemed to do his best stuff when he was down. His words roused the passions and the committed enthusiasm of a multitude of Trust Seekers. In the face of adversity, Paul declared that regardless of whatever he suffered, he remained contented and determined to press forward. His focus was on what he could do to make Christ known to everyone he came in contact with and live the best life possible.

As we press forward, there are some key lessons to remember to gain ground during the transformation process.

Chapter 3: The Heart of the Matter

Lesson #1: Forgive

Many times, we can't move on because we haven't let go of what someone did or said to us, either recently or years ago. We became bitter and fearful; we are quick to distrust and accuse others. The important thing is to begin the process of forgiveness right away. Say aloud, "I forgive ___ for ___." You may not feel anything immediately. In fact, it may feel like a farce for quite a while, but keep saying it to yourself. You have to get your mind set on the act of forgiveness, and then, the feelings will follow. This includes forgiving yourself for any part you may have played in the situation. Whenever feelings or memories resurface say, "No, no. I've forgiven and given it to God." And believe me, feelings will resurface, usually very frequently and powerfully at the beginning, but as time passes, they will become less frequent and less powerful. Also, guilt and condemnation are the works of the enemy to keep you tethered to your past. You can't complete your destiny if you are weighed down by remorse and the enemy knows this. Remember, your contribution to this world and the furtherance of God's Kingdom can be inhibited by your past. Forgive others, forgive yourself, seek God's forgiveness and allow yourself to be free.

Lesson #2: Let It All Out

You have got to release all the pain and hurt that you are feeling. If not, they will linger in your heart and mold you into something other than your true self.

Do you remember reading Great Expectations in high school Literature class? One of the central characters was the extremely eccentric Miss Havisham, who deserves a novel all to herself; her tale is so intriguing. In the story, Miss Havisham was left standing at the altar by her fiancé. She was so heartbroken that she sat in a dilapidated mansion for many years, still dressed in her wedding gown — now tattered and aged — with a towering wedding cake that was gathering cobwebs on the table.

Chapter 3: The Heart of the Matter

The now wizened Miss Havisham was so distraught at the betrayal of her groom that she adopted a beautiful orphaned girl and raised her to have a heart of stone towards any man who showed interest in her. This was her attempt to live vicariously through Estella and exact revenge for the wrong that had been done to her years prior.

Dickens' depiction of this character shows a woman who is jilted by her true love and cannot seem to move forward. Her broken heart renders her incapable of fully giving her heart away again, even to her adopted daughter. Her bitterness is contagious and proliferates itself to those who come in contact with her. She loses touch with reality and remains grounded in the past.

Mourning and grieving are not weaknesses in and of themselves. They are mechanisms used to refresh our goals and prepare us to move on to the next point in our journeys. During my times of grief, I've cried in the shower, screamed at the top of my lungs in the car, and laid belly down/arms

Chapter 3: The Heart of the Matter

sprawled on the floor, soaking the carpet with my tears. I can't say I relished these acts — I wanted nothing more than to just bury the whole thing deep inside of me, but I knew from past experiences and observing others that things that are buried tend to resurface at the most inopportune times. You have to let it out or it will devour your very soul. Take the time to have "great expectations" of the restoration that lies on the other side of the tears.

Lesson #3: Let your "Mess" Become Your "Message."

After King David was confronted with the fact that his adulterous relationship with Bathsheba did not go unnoticed by God, he had to face the swift reality of the consequences for his sin through the death of the child that they had conceived. David tore his clothing, covered himself with ashes, fasted and prayed as a desperate act of repentance. He moaned and pleaded with God, but when the child died, David got up, washed himself, worshiped God, put on his kingly robes and ate a good meal. He then went into Bathsheba to comfort her.

Chapter 3: The Heart of the Matter

Anyone that saw David in the throes of grief would have been astounded at how rapidly he moved through the healing process. His attitude and actions spoke volumes. He did not sulk, curse God, or live in eternal shame. He moved forward with a greater connection to his best friend, and in doing so, he ministers to us in our suffering.

We can learn that we are not to become hopeless victims of our circumstances. We are to become empowered as we gain strength by journeying on. Also, we need to show others who travel similar paths that though the road may be rocky and seemingly bleak, that they can definitely survive and thrive to become victors.

Chapter 4

Out of the Deep

The last heartbreak I went through nearly took me out. All I wanted to do day-in and day-out was lie in bed with the pillow over my head and the blackout curtains covering the windows. My daughter was much younger then, so I knew I couldn't do that and I tried to put on a good face for her. Yet, I didn't laugh, it was more than a little difficult to think "happy thoughts," and I was constantly sighing out loud as I listened to Satan pummel me with one lie after another. At the time, I didn't know they were lies because the words seemed to reveal the underlying truth of my life — I was pitiful and worthless.

Chapter 4: Out of Deep

Depression set in like a heavy weight. I was broken and felt there was no way to put me back together again. My emotions were tapped out, and I trudged through life in a weary cadence. Life, as I knew it, was bleak and there was no hope of recovery in sight.

> *Do not fret because of those who are evil or be envious of those who do wrong; for like the grass they will soon wither, like green plants, they will soon die away.*
>
> *Trust in the Lord and do good; dwell in the land and enjoy safe pasture.*
>
> *Take delight in the Lord, and he will give you the desires of your heart.*
>
> *Commit your way to the Lord; trust in him, and he will do this: He will make your righteous reward shine like the dawn, your vindication like the noonday sun.*
>
> *Be still before the Lord and wait patiently for him;*

*do not fret when people succeed in
their ways, when they carry out their
wicked schemes. (Psalm 37:1-7)*

D is for Depression

I was being assaulted from every angle. It was later that I came to realize that my enemy aimed to use the pain I was feeling to catapult me into a sea of rejection, worthlessness, condemnation, and hopelessness, from which I would never emerge. From Satan's point of view, it's inconsequential to him what apparatus he uses for our torture. He will use any and every person or situation that becomes available as a vessel from which to execute his attack. His objective is to utterly defeat us by destroying any chance of full recovery and ultimately blocking our relationship with God and any chance we have at eternal life. Statistics revealing the current state of our society demonstrate the effectiveness of his plan.

- Within the last twenty years, suicide has increased exponentially in every age group and particularly for teens and women.[1]

Chapter 4: Out of Deep

- Daily about 110 people in the U.S. end their own lives, and around 3,500 attempt suicide.[2]
- More than 42.5 million adults have been diagnosed with a mental illness.[3]
- Every minute nearly twenty people experience some sort of domestic violence.[4]
- Self-harm through cutting and other forms of self-inflicted injuries are escalating. It is believed that one in every 200 teen girls inflict some sort of wound to their bodies daily.[5]
- According to Psychology Today, a National Health Interview Survey reveals that nine percent of adults in the U.S. feel hopeless.[6]

These are just a few of the many statistics that show how the devil is working sadistically to undermine the redemptive process of our Creator.

When we go through intense moments of anger, the depression that meets us at the end can be overwhelming. The darkness of this emotion

Chapter 4: Out of Deep

morphs from what first appears to be a tiny blemish into the never-ending, black abyss spread out in every direction before us. As we plunge head-first into this dark pit, our emotions experience immense claustrophobia as they become squeezed between the negativity of our thoughts and feelings. There seems to be no end to the downward spiral and help seems so far away.

Yet, we have this promise: *[9] Have I not commanded you? Be strong and courageous. Do not be afraid; do not be discouraged, for the LORD your God will be with you wherever you go"* (Joshua 1:9). But the concept of God being totally there with us seems like a foreign concept during the methodical smothering of whatever faith we have while we're going through our tough times. We curl up in the fetal position, too tired to struggle any longer, content to let the hammer fall where it may and praying God would have mercy on our souls.

Chapter 4: Out of Deep

These Are the Days of Elijah

The cheerful tune of the popular gospel song "Days of Elijah" fails to convey one of the darkest times in the Prophet Elijah's life. Fresh from the exuberance of praying to the one true God of Heaven, Elijah was heavy with the victory of seeing God's people return to worshipping Him. This was after the failed attempt of the prophets of Baal to reach their god, Elijah successfully calling fire from Heaven, and the subsequent slaying of Jezebel's prophets. To top this off, Elijah invoked God to end the three-and-a-half year drought that assailed Israel. He was so stoked that he ran ahead of Ahab's chariot as the drenching rain came down (1 Kings 18).

It wasn't long before things took a turn for the worse. When Jezebel heard what had happened to her prophets, she was furious. She swore that Elijah would soon meet the same fate. That's when Elijah's faith and confidence deflated like a balloon. The heights of victory rapidly became the agony of defeat. His overload of emotions came to a screeching halt, and he went on the run.

We all experience times like these when everything is happening one after the other with such intensity that it brings on a feeling of disorientation. Something unexpected suddenly interrupts our journeys and slows us down to a complete stop. We fall into a slump and can do nothing more than rest and heal.

> The Bible says:
> *Then he lay down under the bush and fell asleep.*
> *All at once an angel touched him and said, "Get up and eat." He looked around, and there by his head was some bread baked over hot coals and a jar of water. He ate and drank and then lay down again.*
> *[7]The angel of the L*ORD *came back a second time and touched him and said, "Get up and eat, for the jour-*

Chapter 4: Out of Deep

ney is too much for you." ⁸ So he got up and ate and drank. Strengthened by that food, he traveled forty days and forty nights until he reached Horeb, the mountain of God." (1 Kings 19:5-8)

God personally ministered to Elijah during the time of his must intense dejection. Though he wanted to lay there under the tree in despondency and slip away into eternal rest, God had other plans for him. The angel of the Lord was persistent in seeing that Elijah had sustenance. He even states that he realizes that "*the journey is too much for him*" (see 1 Kings 19:7) as He takes care of all Elijah's needs with shelter (tree), food, and water.

God wants to do the same for you. He wants to shelter you. He will cover you with His feathers, and under His wings, you will find refuge. His faithfulness will be your shield and rampart" (see Psalm 91:4). He knows how much we can take and when life becomes too much for us. *"For He knows how we are formed, he remembers that we are dust"* (Psalms 103:14). He uses some of the darkest times in our lives to reset and restore us. It is in our weakened states that His strength is enhanced (2 Corinthians 12:9).

The Necessity of Change

Depression signals the beginning of a major shift in our lives. There are times when our spirits sense a change approaching from the distance, but a part of us wants to resist. We cling to the familiar, though what's familiar may be showing signs of wear and erosion. We want more, newer, better and yet, we don't want the cost of pursuing change. We hunker down, hoping that things will get better, with little to no discomfort on our parts.

If you've ever gone through a remodeling of a house or any space you've spent time in, there is a lot of noise, debris, and clutter you have to put up with during the modification of that space. Depending on the length of time for completion of the project, you may find yourself feeling overwhelmed with the inconvenience of reconstruction. Some people even become so frustrated that they want to give up mid-project, wanting stuff to go back to the way it was — back to normal; back to what was once acceptable. Any transition can be uncomfortable, but once the long-awaited transformation is complete, the satisfaction we experience is exhilarating and makes us happy to put up with the annoyance.

Everything within us shuns the idea that times of distress will eventually lead to times of jubilation, but the word of God promises exactly that (see Romans 8:28). We have to fall back on what we know with our whole heart regarding how things usually turn out while the Father takes care of us. If you don't know, let Psalms 91:1-16 remind you.

> *Whoever dwells in the shelter of the Most High will rest in the shadow of the Almighty. I will say of the LORD, "He is my refuge and my fortress, my God, in whom I trust. "Surely he*

*will save you from the fowler's snare
and from the deadly pestilence.
He will cover you with his feathers,
and under his wings you will find
refuge; his faithfulness will be your
shield and rampart.
You will not fear the terror of night,
nor the arrow that flies by day, nor
the pestilence that stalks in the darkness, nor the plague that destroys at
midday.
A thousand may fall at your side, ten
thousand at your right hand, but it
will not come near you. You will only
observe with your eyes and see the
punishment of the wicked. If you say,
"The LORD is my refuge," and you
make the Most High your dwelling,
no harm will overtake you, no disaster will come near your tent.
For he will command his angels concerning you to guard you in all your
ways; they will lift you up in their*

*hands, so that you will not strike
your foot against a stone.
You will tread on the lion and the cobra; you will trample the great lion
and the serpent.
"Because he loves me," says
the* LORD, *"I will rescue him; I will
protect him, for he acknowledges my
name.
He will call on me, and I will answer
him; I will be with him in trouble, I
will deliver him and honor him.
With long life I will satisfy him and
show him my salvation."* (Psalms 91)

God loves you deeply, passionately, and is looking forward to spending an eternity with you. He is your true source of security, and you can count on Him to shelter you from whatever storm you're going through. For instance, imagine being stuck outside during a storm. You run towards the shelter. Along the way you are splattered with mud, drenched by the rain, surrounded by thunder and tormented by lightning strikes. You finally reach the shelter. You're still surrounded by the storm, you've experienced some chaos, but now, your refuge keeps you safe from being wildly tossed to and fro. Your faith in the goodness and promises of God should steady you at all times and shine a light of hope, reminding you that your rescue is imminent.

The Key

The time to immerse yourself in His word is now—when you don't feel like praying or thinking about anything of the spiritual nature. You must be aware that the enemy uses times of hopelessness to destroy any connection that we may have with God. Our faith is crushed, and he wants it to die on the ground where it lies in the belief that it can never be resuscitated. But these are also the times when God speaks to us through that still, small voice. He may influence a stranger to say something to you that shifts your thinking or He may direct you to a book that contains thoughts so profound they singe your mind like molten lava, affecting the very way you are living at this point in your life.

Chapter 4: Out of Deep

Even though I didn't want to seek the Lord during my deep depression, He pursued me and began enlightening me to His will and His ways. Books and articles I read piqued my interest, causing me to want to discover more of what God says in His word and absorb any advice that would help me to push forward. The lies that the enemy whispered to me were quickly refuted through a sermon that, amazingly, fit my exact situation. The enemy had been telling me that happiness was not for me because I was just not one of the "chosen ones" who have everything work out for them all the time. I soon understood why he is called the "father of lies". But his power was quickly diminished due to the loving persistence of my Heavenly Father.

Reading God's word brought forth a desire for me to change. I wanted to be whole again. Not the same as I was before, but better. I was no longer comfortable being as I was, so I ravenously devoured all that the Holy Spirit led me to in order to find my way to the new me. I had the intense longing to know God as my constant companion. I then

Chapter 4: Out of Deep

became stronger and set on a path to have the abundant life He promises in John 10:10.

So, the key is take this time to rest and be very gentle with yourself. Place yourself in God's hands. He will nourish you, shield you, and soothe your wounded soul. He will bring freshness to the atmosphere surrounding you, a freshness that will revive your senses and your soul. And He will guide you where you need to be in your thinking and experiences when you are ready to be exposed to them. Strive to discover authors and online ministries who compel you to listen for the voice of God as you learn to tamp down the voice of the enemy.

You will recover. Just remember: you've got all of Heaven at your disposal, and you will make some amazing discoveries about yourself and God at this time if you just rest in Him.

Chapter 4: Out of Deep

Notes

1. *Tavernise, S. (2018). U.S. Suicide Rate Surges to a 30-Year High. [online] Nytimes.com. Available at: https://www.nytimes.com/2016/04/22/health/us-suicide-rate-surges-to-a-30-year-high.html [Accessed 6 August 2017].*
2. *Hope for Depression. (2018). Facts about Depression | Hope for Depression. [online] Available at: https://www.hopefordepression.org/depression-facts/ [Accessed 6 August 2017].*
3. *Newsweek. (2018). Nearly 1 in 5 Americans Suffer From Mental Illness Each Year. [online] Available at: http://www.newsweek.com/nearly-1-5-americans-suffer-mental-illness-each-year-230608 [Accessed 6 August 2017].*
4. *Ncadv.org. (2018). NCADV | National Coalition Against Domestic Violence. [online] Available at: https://ncadv.org/statistics [Accessed 6 August 2017].*

5. *Teen Help. (2018). Cutting Statistics and Self-Injury Treatment - Teen Help. [online] Available at: https://www.teenhelp.com/physical-health/cutting-statistics-and-self-injury-treatment/ [Accessed 6 August 2017].*
6. *Psychology Today. (2018). Sad, Worthless, Hopeless? [online] Available at: https://www.psychologytoday.com/blog/how-everyone-became-depressed/201406/sad-worthless-hopeless [Accessed 6 August 2017].*

Chapter 5
My Personal Apocalypse

There was a specific moment when I realized that the battle I experiencing was also happening in the spiritual realm. I was fighting *"not against flesh and blood, but against principalities…"* (Ephesians 6:12).

I remember one night in particular, I had a very restless sleep. I dreamt about torturous moments from my past — words that were said to me that deeply wounded me, and imagined things that could or could not be occurring with those who betrayed me. I was certain that behind the scenes, my betrayers were living the good life and laughing at my discomfort.

Chapter 5: My Personal Apocalypse

My dreams or nightmares as they were, seemed so intense that I began crying in my sleep. The sobs were so heartfelt that I woke up and continued to bemoan my situation. I was lying on my stomach when I heard a thump at the bedroom door as if someone had pushed it back towards the wall. I rolled over, thinking it was my daughter awakened by my crying. It was not, but what I saw caused me to draw in a sharp breath.

There, in the doorway, stood a shadowy figure. I couldn't really see any distinguishing features, but I saw its shadow cast on the door from the light dim light coming from the kitchen. The figure seemed to have a hat on, and it was pointed in my direction.

I quickly jumped out of bed, but the figure fled before I could turn on the lights. Right then, I knew that there were spirits in the room which were set on tormenting me through the night.

Chapter 5: My Personal Apocalypse

I was confused and too weak to do anything but sit up and keep watch all night. I checked on my child, but her sleep seemed undisturbed. I prayed a little bit, but as I said before, I didn't think I could get a prayer through. God had left me, I was sure, and I was at the mercy of whatever was trying to take over my mind. There was nothing I could do and no one to talk to about what I experienced— especially at that hour.

I knew what my family would say. They would brush it off and try to convince me that what I saw was not really there — that my mind was playing tricks on me. I definitely did not feel far from losing my mind, but I knew what I'd seen, and I was convinced that the devil was trying to first destroy my mind before completely destroying me.

Looking back, I realized that there was quite a bit of spiritual warfare surrounding my family and me during this time. My daughter often saw dark figures running through the house or standing in the

Chapter 5: My Personal Apocalypse

kitchen. One night, just before I drifted off to sleep, I had the very strong sensation of someone wrapping their arms around me from behind. Things began breaking and falling apart (representative of me, I guess) and there seemed to be an infestation of bugs that appeared out of nowhere. One night, I woke up in a fit of coughing. From the dim light that entered the room, it looked as if I was surrounded by thick smoke. When I got out of bed, turned on the light, and walked around the house all was well.

As I drew farther from God, more and more bad things happened. But I didn't care. I'd always been good; dedicated to helping people in anyway I could, committed to going to church and praying, always trying to do my best. And all He had for me was trial after trial, disappointment after disappointment, heartache after heartache.

God didn't care about me, so I was going to be the only way I knew how to be—neutral.

Chapter 5: My Personal Apocalypse

Come to find out "neutral" is not really neutral. If you don't choose the side of God, you are automatically choosing the side of the devil. There is no sitting on the fence spiritually. You are either for God or for the enemy.

And don't think that the devil makes it easy either. His job, as the thief, is to "steal, kill, and destroy." He steals whatever happiness and life you might have, he kills the hopes and dreams you've been striving for, and he destroys your life slowly and methodically.

Yet, I was convinced that God had it out for me; that maybe sometime in my past I'd done something so bad that He was set on taking every opportunity He could to get back at me. A lot of people think of God as a "get you back God," and they keep running away from Him as a result. It is difficult to realize that He is a God full of unconditional love and grace. He wants to take care of us and bring us out of any pit that we've dug for ourselves. God does convict us of what we are doing

Chapter 5: My Personal Apocalypse

that is contrary to his will. He brings to light the things done in the dark, but He doesn't do it to get back at us. He wants to expose us to the guilt and shame hidden in our hearts so that we can begin to heal and travel down the right road as we turn our lives over to Him.

> *Do not make light of the Lord's discipline, and do not lose heart when he rebukes you because the Lord disciplines those he loves and he punishes everyone he accepts as a son (or daughter). Endure hardship as discipline; God is treating you as sons (daughters). For what son is not disciplined by his father? If you are not disciplined (and everyone undergoes discipline), then you are illegitimate children and not true sons.* Hebrews 12:5-8

It's the end of time. Natural phenomena are occurring every day that perplex the most scientific of minds. People are becoming more callused and

Chapter 5: My Personal Apocalypse

despondent; horrendous and unthinkable events occur that leave a slew of broken hearts and torn lives trailing behind.

Satan realizes his time is short and his objective is to burden every soul with feelings of hopelessness and despair. As he operates in the unseen realm, we often see the results of his work. But God is at work too. We must remember that He has told us the end of the story, and in this battle of good vs. evil, good will definitely win.

Our job is to focus on doing what is right and to believe that God is committed to helping us make it through. He doesn't leave us floundering alone, trying to figure it all out without a hint as to what we should do. We must begin by taking the first steps towards transformation, and God will take over by freeing us from shame, guilt, grief, fear, doubt, and iniquity in general. Take steps to allow Him to "create in (you) a clean heart and renew the right spirit within you."

Chapter 5: My Personal Apocalypse

The Whole Armor

Put on the full armor of God, so that you can take your stand against the devil's schemes. For our struggle is not against flesh and blood, but against the rulers, against the authorities, against the powers of this dark world and against the spiritual forces of evil in the heavenly realms.
Ephesians 6:11-12

When I was a little girl, I was quite the history buff. I loved to read books set in the past—it didn't matter what time period. Stories about kings and queens, peasants and tyrants, knights and knaves all intrigued me. I've always been impressed by the tenacity of the human spirit in the face of adversity and oppression.

I'd look at people like Oskar Schindler, and his incredible ingenuity in creating a list of Jewish laborers for his factory in Germany which helped save over one thousand of those Jews from extermi-

Chapter 5: My Personal Apocalypse

nation in the Auschwitz Death Camp. Or Harriett Tubman who, after narrowly escaping slavery in the South, returned many times to help lead over one hundred slaves to freedom. These people and others sacrificed themselves and their families to stand against the atrocities committed by fellow humans.

There seems to be no end to the amount of terrible things people will do to one another. It is astounding how many crimes are committed today by people who have no regrets and show absolutely no remorse. Not long ago, a friend wrote a Facebook post in near hysterics about the shocking murder of an older gentleman broadcast on Facebook Live by behavioral health agent, Steve Stephens. Stephens was angry with a girlfriend who had broken up with him and moved on. He quit his job and soon decided to go on a killing rampage, during which he took the life of a seventy-four-year-old grandfather who had just left one of his family member's homes after having Easter dinner. The unsuspecting victim was shot down in cold blood on

Chapter 5: My Personal Apocalypse

the live internet as Stephens taunted him to say his ex-girlfriend's name. Stephens later shot himself as he was being pursued by police. The repercussions of his destructive behavior ended the life of his victim and changed the life of his ex-girlfriend.

There is something insidious in the atmosphere. People are becoming more selfish and self-centered every day. Many are indifferent in regards to any offense they may make towards another, whether small or big. The prevailing mindset is "it's all about me," and humanity is becoming more brittle and unstable emotionally, as a result.

You may be like me; a person who feels things deeply. One who knows that behind every word or action is an indication of what lies in the heart of a person.

Or perhaps you've set your eyes on a hero; someone you admire and respect; someone who seems infallible only to have your heart broken as they disappoint you when their hidden betrayal

Chapter 5: My Personal Apocalypse

comes to light.

It is difficult at times to remember that mere mortal man cannot sustain the weight of your worship. No one on this Earth can sustain you, take care of all your needs, and love as completely as the One who made you. Jesus is the only one who has lived here who was perfect. He is the one who now oversees every detail of your life to bring out the best results. He is our Strong Tower, our Protector, and our Deliverer.

In His role as your protector, Jesus has provided an arsenal of tools, including the full armor, which is at your disposal to help you as you stand against the things which are happening around you that seem bizarre and irrational. Whenever you are feeling overwhelmed with life in general focus on the promises in Psalms 91. Throughout the chapter, God describes all the high tech security available under Him. He is a well-fortified castle that has impenetrable walls. In His arms is

Chapter 5: My Personal Apocalypse

safety. No matter what problems may assail you, no matter how many problems come your way, God is fully capable of protecting you from all of them.

Since we live in a world full of sin, the enemy's job is to make sure that you have flaming arrows flung your way. The devil wants you to succumb to the fear and anxiety that pounds like a battering ram on your castle door. Yet, remember that your Fortress stands firm and is able to withhold any attack the enemy may come at you with. You will remain unscathed, and the castle will stand--unbreachable.

God has promised never to leave you or forsake you (Hebrews 13:5). There is no one like Him as He is the only one who loves you with an everlasting love (Jeremiah 31.3). You can count on the Lord to love you and take care of you through it all. Think about it: There is nowhere you can go and nowhere that you can hide that He is not there waiting for you with open arms.

Chapter 5: My Personal Apocalypse

Where can I go from your Spirit?
Where can I flee from your
presence?
If I go up to the heavens, you are
there; if I make my bed in the depths,
you are there.
If I rise on the wings of the dawn, if I
settle on the far side of the sea, even
there your hand will guide me,
your right hand will hold me fast. If I
say, Surely the darkness will hide
me and the light become night
around me," even the darkness will
not be dark to you; the night will
shine like the day, for darkness is as
light to you.
For you created my inmost be-
ing; you knit me together in my
mother's womb.—Psalms 139:7-13

God loves you. He knew you before your parents realized you were even a possibility. He knows where you've been, where you are going and every other detail of your life. Commit yourself to Him. Give your heart to Him. You will be completely safe in His arms.

Chapter 6
The Formula

Elisha said to Gehazi, "Tuck your cloak into your belt, take my staff in your hand and run. Don't greet anyone you meet, and if anyone greets you, do not answer. Lay my staff on the boy's face." (2 Kings 4:29)

There was a period of time in the midst of my transformation when all I wanted to do was find the key — the right words to charm God into doing whatever I needed Him to do — get me to my breakthrough quick, fast, and in a hurry. I felt that I'd suffered through my internal pain of heartbreak and rejection far longer than was necessary. My mind kept repeating all the hurtful scenes and the echo of the devastating words were embedded in my ears on constant replay. I'd had enough. I just wanted to get it over with immediately, but the pain didn't seem to be budging. What could I say to move the hand of God faster? What were the magic words? Was there something I needed to do to help the process along? Maybe to go to church more, read one more chapter of the Bible, or listen to one more gospel song. I needed the formula to cure all my woes.

In the above verse, Elisha prescribes a formula to resurrect the young son of the Shunammite woman. If you don't know the story, read the entire chapter of 2 Kings 4. In summary, it tells the story of a wealthy woman who was a benefactor of the prophet Elisha. Apparently, she and her husband were so fond of the prophet that they built a room attached above their home where he could rest from his journeys between towns and ministering.

Chapter 6: The Formula

The prophet, out of appreciation, asked the woman what she wanted in return for her generosity. She said there was nothing she needed or wanted. Gehazi, Elisha's assistant, reminded the prophet that the woman had no child and that her husband was up in age. So, the prophet promised her that she would give birth the next year. The Shunammite woman plead with him not to trifle with her. She did not want to get her hopes up and her heart set on something that she'd come to grips long ago would not happen. But give birth, she did. The boy grew, and a few years later, during harvest time, the boy complained of a headache while out in the fields with his father. When he returned home, he died on his mother's lap.

The woman laid the boy's body on the bed of the prophet and traveled to Mount Caramel to speak with him. As she was a long ways off, Elisha spotted her coming towards him. He sent his assistant out to meet her, and when asked the reason for her visit, her only reply was, "All is well."

Chapter 6: The Formula

When she reached the prophet, she threw herself at his feet, admonishing him for giving her what she did not ask for in the first place, only to be disappointed by losing the gift anyway.

Elisha came up with what he thought was a quick and sure remedy. Gehazi was to go ahead and administer the prescription. His instructions were simple. Elisha gave Gehazi the step-by-step directions to dispense the cure. It all seemed foolproof, but it was not to be. The mother told the prophet that she would not leave him until he took care of this situation himself. Good thing she did. The formula, at first, did not work and the boy remained dead. It took a lot of prayer and time to bring the boy back.

The same could be said of my dilemma. I was looking for the five-step plan for getting better quicker — nothing too involving and definitely nothing too long. The right words — an incantation of sorts that would bring closure to my situation and help me move on with life as I knew it.

Chapter 6: The Formula

The Process of Change

I wish I could just write you a handy-dandy bullet-list of the things you should do to ensure your complete healing. You know, like those articles in the women's magazines that promise you weight loss, complete joy, or the perfect marriage in just five easy steps. True transformation is not that simple. There is no prescription that the doctor can send to the pharmacy to be filled as your cure-all. After all, a good marriage, self-acceptance, and unspeakable joy cannot be realized in just a few simple steps, or even through some magic pill. Removing yourself from the physical, spiritual, and emotional limbo you are in will take some thought and action on your part. God and all the forces of heaven will be there to assist you at all times, but you must take the first step in each area of the process and commit yourself to be open to what the Lord may reveal. There may be weaknesses in you that you have been trying to cover up and it needs to come out. There may be unresolved issues from your past that need to come to light so that both you and God can deal with them. You may need to peel away the layers of past hurts and disappointments — choices that were not influenced by God — to get to the heart of the matter. You will be taken out of your comfort zone. There's no question about that. You may make a 180-degree change in everything about yourself. Those who know you will cast you questionable looks, but that's alright. This is all about TRANSFORMING. When something transforms, it doesn't stay completely the same. Sure, there may be some similarities to who you were in the past, but there is something that is different that diverges away from the norm.

So, are you ready? Take it slow. Just dip your toes in to test the waters before you jump in. After all, you have a loving Father who has the remedy for what ails you. He's not going anywhere. He'll help to guide you through where you're going and never let you go.

Chapter 7

Going Where You Don't Want to Go and Doing What You Don't Want to Do

There have been times when my daughter, Alyx, has had to do something she really, really didn't want to do. For example, when she had to present a project in front of her class at school, or when she had to graciously thank someone for a gift she felt was undeserving of thanks. For instance, during a gift exchange, Alyx received a box of chocolate-covered cherries from the person who picked her name while she gave her person a beautiful necklace. She was beyond disappointed, and I could feel her pain. But what she didn't realize was that the little girl who purchased her gift was recently placed in a foster home while her mom

Chapter 7: Going Where You Don't Want to Go and Doing What You Don't Want to Do

was in rehab recovering from extreme drug abuse. I knew, so I asked her to tell the girl "thank you." The tears started to flow, and she said, "But Mamma, I don't wanna." I put my arms around her shoulders and told her, "Well, you have to do it because it's the right thing to do, so suck those tears up and do what you have to do."

When our pain threshold is at an all-time high and we feel like we've been terribly wronged, it can be difficult to extricate ourselves from the emotional pit we've dug to hide in. We sit in darkness, holding our knees and rocking back and forth, focused on what could have been, what should have been, and how everything is supposed to be. Our dysfunction cripples us to the point where moving forward seems too hard, and staying where we are binds us up and smothers the life out of us. We become so fixated on our pain that it consumes us to no end. There seems to be nothing else in our lives that matters other than what we are feeling at that very moment. This is the time we cannot afford to let our souls become overburdened

Chapter 7: Going Where You Don't Want to Go and Doing What You Don't Want to Do

with the adversities of life. We must resolve to be "more than conquerors" (Romans 8:37), gird our loins, and do what we have to do to heal.

Chloe, our beautiful golden-colored Chihuahua, developed a hot spot right inside her left back leg during the summer. The spot was very red and inflamed all the time. It was absolutely irritated. We bathed her constantly to keep her cool, repeatedly moisturized the inflamed area and put ointment on the spot, but Chloe would not leave it alone! She would sit for hours, if we let her, licking and nursing the spot, effectively removing anything we'd put on it to help it heal. Whenever we caught her in her fixation, we'd tell her to stop, and she would, but only for a short amount of time. Later, she would be back at it, making the area more raw and irritated with each lick.

Do you see the analogy between what Chloe does and what we're doing to ourselves? We take our wounds and pick at them until they become aggravated enough to develop into open sores. Pus-

Chapter 7: Going Where You Don't Want to Go and Doing What You Don't Want to Do

filled and oozing, the tender spots become more chafed as we poke at them to see if they are still sensitive. We stockpile every offense, every breach of trust, every difficulty that has come our way and hoard them like Ebenezer Scrooge did his coins. After this, we reflect upon the wrongdoing and ruminate upon it continuously. We become consumed with everything that happened; our imaginations get away from us, and all we think, breath, and do is influenced by the incident that caused the wound to occur. You cannot go on like this forever. You must come to the point where you decide that enough is enough. You've got to set your mind to move on.

You do yourself a great disservice when you take all your memories, broken dreams, offenses, injustices and hold them close to your heart. The healing only begins when you loosen your grip and let it go. This is the time when you must tell yourself some truths. It doesn't matter whether your pain comes from a job that was terminated, a business that deflated, or a romance that fizzled.

Chapter 7: Going Where You Don't Want to Go and Doing What You Don't Want to Do

You've got to come to terms with the circumstance surrounding your time of emotional torment.

Are you holding on because you are romanticizing the situation? Was it really all you drummed it up to be in your mind? Was there something you did or didn't do to contribute to the demise of the relationship, job or opportunity? If so, face up to it, talk with God about it, and forgive yourself. You need to forgive yourself so there won't be any self-deprecation or condemnation. We all have battles we fight every day, and sometimes, we fall. But the key to remember during these times is not to stay down in a low place, defeated (Proverbs 24:16). You are victorious because we have unwavering help from the Father.

Make a resolute decision now to commit yourself to your healing. *"Cast all your anxiety on him because he cares for you"* (1 Peter 5:7). Casting takes you to the first level of healing. Turning it over to God releases you from tormenting thoughts— thoughts that cause you to

Chapter 7: Going Where You Don't Want to Go and Doing What You Don't Want to Do

think you have some sort of self-imposed responsibility to do something to receive vindication or reparations for what you've been through. It gives God the freedom to work within your life to help work everything out for good. Until you cast your problems upon Him, God can do nothing about your situation because you are trying to do everything in your own power. Some people may say, "I've done this all before. I've asked God to take all of it away. I cast all the time, but He's just not listening. He doesn't hear me. I'm just sitting here miserable, but God doesn't care about me at all."

I can relate. There have been times when I've prayed, pleaded, asked God to talk to me, show me what to do, or send me a sign. I've even dropped my Bible and asked Him to let it fall open to a verse that would inspire me. That's usually when it fell on the begats! Maybe there was a sign in that, but I just wasn't getting it. I even went so far as to do the Gideon thing — in Judges 6:36-38, Gideon was given a message from an angel of the

Chapter 7: Going Where You Don't Want to Go and Doing What You Don't Want to Do

Lord. In order to make sure he had heard it right, he put a fleece on the ground, and if it was either wet or dry after two nights, he reasoned within himself that he had his answer from the Lord. I tried the same thing with a washcloth. Nothing happened.

While I sat there trying to devise my next strategy to hear a word from God, I grew more and more frustrated — more doubtful. Was there even a God to hear my prayers? What if this proves that anything spiritual is just a big hoax? Well, whatever. If someone is up there, He sure isn't listening to me! It was during this time of intense doubt that I began to dabble with some of the dark arts — by consulting psychics and toying with the occult. I will go into detail in my next book, but suffice it to say that this time of despair was a time that shook my faith to the very core, and the attacks of the enemy distracted me so much from God's will that I almost forfeited not only my destiny, but the destinies of my family. The enemy was really working overtime on me! He took a lifetime of beliefs and childlike faith and tried to shatter them

Chapter 7: Going Where You Don't Want to Go and Doing What You Don't Want to Do

into a million pieces in one fell swoop. I could almost feel him gloating, saying, "I've got her now," while rubbing his hands together in maniacal glee.

That's when I heard it. It was a slight whisper —steady, yet, almost imperceptible. The voices of confusion were so loud in my head that it was almost drowned out. Yet, though it was faint, it was unyielding. The voice said, "Be still. I am here" over and over again. Like Superman, I strained to block out all the other voices of derision and honed into that small sound. That was the turning point for me—focusing on that still, small voice.

From that point forward, I prayed constantly. I prayed in the car. I prayed doing dishes. I prayed in the shower. I prayed under my breath while I was teaching. I prayed and prayed every time thoughts of my pain resurfaced or negative images assaulted my mind. There were times I would shout to the Lord, asking Him why things were in such

Chapter 7: Going Where You Don't Want to Go and Doing What You Don't Want to Do

upheaval. What did I do wrong? What sins had I or anyone in my family committed that I was being forced to pay for? What in the world was going on? As I shouted to the Lord, I cried—deep, heart-wrenching wails. I blubbered and snorted and blustered and blew until I was spent. Funny thing is, after going through such volatile sessions, a certain peace passed over me. It was as if God had His hand around me, lovingly embracing me and saying, "There, there. It's going to be alright."

Oh, but the enemy was relentless. He would put a song on the radio or have someone say something that would make my heart clench tightly in my chest. But try as he might, I had heard the voice of God, and there was no stopping my pursuit of Him! I would start my prayer session over again. Every time a thought or fear reignited itself, I would take it to the Lord to handle.

It doesn't matter if you have to pray every ten seconds for God to soothe your wounded heart. It doesn't matter if it seems no time elapses from one mental assault to the other. Our foe is not one to give up easily. He has had centuries of experience, and we are merely dust to him. How do we fight against powers from the spiritual realm that are intent on taking our very souls?

> *For we wrestle not against flesh and blood, but against principalities, against powers, against the rulers of the darkness of this world, against spiritual wickedness in high places. Wherefore take unto you the whole armor of God, that ye may be able to withstand in the evil day, and having done all, to stand.*
>
> *Stand therefore, having your loins girt about with truth, and having on the breastplate of righteousness;*
>
> *And your feet shod with the preparation of the gospel of peace;*
>
> *Above all, taking the shield of faith, wherewith ye shall be able to quench all the fiery darts of the wicked.*

Chapter 7: Going Where You Don't Want to Go and Doing What You Don't Want to Do

And take the helmet of salvation, and the sword of the Spirit, which is the word of God. (Ephesians 6:12-17)

As the enemy assails you with fear, doubts, and the temptation to resign from life, protect yourself from his onslaughts with the full armor of God. Reach out to Jesus, give Him your pain, stand still, and let God fight this battle for you (Exodus 14:14). It is then and only then that you will truly be able to sit back and witness the complete deliverance of your life and destiny by the Lord.

Notes

Let me just take a moment to say that my exposure to the world of the occult enlightened me to some of the subtle ways that spiritualism is entering our homes and churches, and how Satan has emboldened the entertainment industry to infiltrate our homes with contempt for the things of God. But that is the topic of my next book.

Chapter 8

Things are Not What They Seem to Be

My friend, Abby, who, before her retirement, used to be a case worker for one of our state agencies, tells the story of a home visit she and her co-worker, Jimmy, made. This was at the home of a client in a rural area just outside of town. She and Jimmy sat down on the sofa in the client's living room, and she began the interview process to complete all the necessary paperwork. As she and the client were talking, Jimmy began snacking on some peanuts that were in a bowl on a nearby sofa table. Abby said that she'd given him a questioning look, but went on with the interview without saying anything. Suddenly, Jimmy interrupted, exclaiming, "Ummm, these sure are some good

Chapter 8: Things are Not What They Seem to Be

peanuts!" The client's face beamed as she gave him a toothless grin and said, "If you think they are good now, you should've had 'em when they had chocolate on them!"

Abby said that Jimmy's face turned ten shades of purple in three seconds, and he abruptly left the sofa to run outside. The interview was definitely over. Abby went on to tell me that Jimmy and all the other caseworkers were warned, off-handedly, not to eat anything from clients' homes — even if they were offered food in the most hospitable way. Yet Jimmy, apparently bored and restless during the interview process, ignored common sense and ate what was sitting within arm's reach.

Life Lesson

We often do the same thing that Jimmy did. The Holy Spirit, in His wisdom, guides us to walk a certain path. This path is designed to help us reject those things which are mere distractions — things that are just sitting there available for our pleasure

Chapter 8: Things are Not What They Seem to Be

whenever we are bored, lonely and looking for excitement. Many things capture our attention like:

- The stranger who instant messages you without warning, weaving intricate tales of his life and how he is interested in getting to know you better.
- The sure-fire business deal that people say is the cash cow you've been looking for. The only thing is that it requires you to invest your life's savings, and you must do this quickly before the opportunity passes.
- Your time surfing the internet has led you to stumble upon one of the most provocative sites on the World Wide Web. You put your hand on the mouse, intending to make a hasty retreat, but your eyes linger on the screen as you hover the arrow over the next link, curious to see what else will pop up.

Things are not always what they appear to be on the surface. Even Satan can appear as an angel of light (2 Corinthian 11:14), but we should be aware of his insidious nature and the devices he

Chapter 8: Things are Not What They Seem to Be

uses to throw us off guard. Peter says it best: *Be sober, be vigilant, because your adversary the devil walketh about as a roaring lion, seeking whom he may devour* (1 Peter 5:8). The enemy wants us to get involved in every issue, every protest, and every problem that presents itself to us so that we can fail to see his sleight-of-hand. We must be observers of everything around us. We should sit back, quiet and prayerful, and watch what goes on around us. Whenever you become an observer of the world, you open up yourself to witness the oddities and inconsistencies that you normally would not see because you have been distracted and desensitized. You begin to develop God-given instincts—instincts that will help you to immediately discern when something or someone is not quite right. When we are involved and operating on full-throttle in the world—becoming immersed in everything and every situation, we often miss clues that can usually be detected through the undercurrent of what is occurring.

So today, be a watcher. Pray for clarity from

Chapter 8: Things are Not What They Seem to Be

the Holy Spirit. Keep your impulses under control. Just step back and discover what mysteries lay beneath the surface because things are not always what they seem to be.

Chapter 9

You Don't Have to Do Life Alone

So let's keep focused on that goal, those of us who want everything God has for us. If any of you have something else in mind, something less than total commitment, God will clear your blurred vision—you'll see it yet! Now that we're on the right track, let's stay on it. Stick with me, friends. Keep track of those you see running this same course, headed for this same goal. There are many out there taking other paths, choosing other goals, and trying to get you to go along with them. I've warned you of them many times; sadly, I'm

Chapter 9: You Don't Have to Do Life Alone

> *having to do it again. All they want is easy street. They hate Christ's Cross. But easy street is a dead-end street. Those who live there make their bellies their gods; belches are their praise; all they can think of is their appetites. But there's far more to life for us. We're citizens of high heaven! We're waiting the arrival of the Savior, the Master, Jesus Christ, who will transform our earthy bodies into glorious bodies like his own. He'll make us beautiful and whole with the same powerful skill by which he is putting everything as it should be, under and around him.*
> Philippians 3:15-21 (MSG)

We had just finished up family night at the small country school I worked at, and Alyx and I were tired. We lived about forty minutes from the school at that time, so we slid into the car for the long ride from the country back to the nearby city

Chapter 9: You Don't Have to Do Life Alone

where we lived. I made sure Alyx was buckled up in her car seat before I backed the car up and started off. It was a winter night that was pitch black, except for the occasional street light, and the stretch was lonely. We were the only car on the road for a while. I did glimpse some headlights behind me at quite a distance. I became lulled by the sounds of the road and drove on at a reasonable speed, ever watchful for the occasional deer that could be found leaping across the highway.

Suddenly, those far away headlights were right up behind me. A large, flat-bed eighteen wheeler came up behind me on the highway very fast. The driver of the truck rode the back of my bumper for a little while, and then, he got into the left lane and passed me, going pretty fast. Unexpectedly, he got back in my lane and put on brakes right in front of me. Had I been just a little more tired and not alert, I would have run right into the back of his flatbed, but I quickly slammed on my brakes, gave a quick tap of my horn, went into the left lane, and passed him by.

Chapter 9: You Don't Have to Do Life Alone

The truck driver flew into the left lane behind me, turned on his bright lights and sped up to catch up with me. I signaled to go back into the slow lane, and he slid over behind me. Glancing at Alyx in the rearview mirror, I could see her eyes shining through the dark with concern. I pushed the pedal down and went faster. I changed lanes. He followed me. I changed lanes again. He did the same. For about fifteen minutes, this crazy driver and I played Chicken down a long, nearly deserted highway in South Carolina. All the way, I breathed a prayer that God would take care of us and keep the deer off of the road that night.

I was sweating profusely, even though the night was chilly. I was scared. Alyx held her hand up from her car seat, I guess in an effort to let our pursuer know there was a child on board. But that trucker was unrelenting in his pursuit of us. He blared his horn as he accelerated even faster behind me. By this time, I was in tears, but I kept driving, fixing my eyes ahead, praying to see the lights of the city. Alyx said, "Momma, what's happening?"

Chapter 9: You Don't Have to Do Life Alone

I replied as calmly as I could while my whole body shook, "Don't worry. Just keep your eyes straight ahead, and look for the city lights."

By this time, I was absolutely positive that the truck driver was demented. He followed me like a crazed maniac for miles until we reached the outskirts of the city. As soon as we entered an area where there were more drivers and street lights, he backed off a bit. When we arrived at a slightly busy intersection, I went over to the farthest left lane. My intention was, when the light turned green, to go down what looked like a busy street to see if he would attempt to follow me home. If he did, I would have driven straight to the police station. He didn't. He remained in the far right lane and pulled up well enough so that I could get a glimpse of his face. He looked down at me with a look of pure indifference. It was as if we never had our bizarre encounter on the highway. If you had seen him, you would have never imagined him being involved in an incident of road rage because he looked so innocent at that moment. I'd imagined some sneering

Chapter 9: You Don't Have to Do Life Alone

lunatic in the cab of that truck. Instead, I stared into the face of serene obliviousness. He didn't care that he almost killed me and my child. He didn't have any remorse for anything. And he would probably subject another unsuspecting driver to his maniacal rage elsewhere on his journey. I prayed a quick prayer that God would send angels before him to protect others on the road. I turned away from him, waited for the light to change, and made my way home.

Years later, when I now recall that night, a lump rises in my throat as I think about what could have happened. If I didn't have hope that bright lights and a thriving town lay just ahead, if I had not stayed focused on the road ahead of me while that maniac bore down on me, I would have become befuddled and confused. Fear would have taken over, and I would have probably made a mistake that would have cost us our lives. But I persevered because I was focused on the hope that lay ahead of me, and I was determined to make it to safety.

Chapter 9: You Don't Have to Do Life Alone

Running into the Unexpected

As we walk through this life, we often happen upon a battle that totally catches us off guard. The enemy slides upon us, and we get caught in his cross-hairs. Suddenly, we are thrown into the ring to fight for our very lives.

In the movie, Independence Day, there is a battle scene near the end where human pilots are in the middle of a melee of alien fighters. The scene flashes into the cockpit of the plane of one of the human pilots as he is looking all around him at the alien aircraft scrambling through the skies. He exclaims in sheer terror, "They're everywhere!" He's then blown to smithereens. Often, we do the same thing as that pilot did; when the enemy is in hot pursuit of us, we pull our gaze from what we should be doing — our mission — and panic when the enemy blitzes us with weapons of mass destruction. Or we may become frozen in our tracks, paralyzed with fear. We glance back at the enemy as he carries out his plan to obliterate us. His assaults begin to provoke and distract us. My main purpose that dark night was to get both Alyx and me home safely. If I had pulled my gaze from the road long enough to stare back at that trucker, I would have become frozen with fear due to the complete overwhelming terror of this surprise, unconscionable attack. He would have annihilated us on the spot. The enemy likes to get out in front of us in the same manner that the trucker got in front of my car. He wants to get in our minds, assailing us with our fears. He longs to distract us just long enough to shake us up and throw us off course. You see, the enemy knows that if you are concentrating on what God would have you to focus on, you will gain the knowledge of how powerful you are through the Holy Spirit, and you will become a downright menace to his plans. So, he takes every opportunity he can to distract you from your goals and, most importantly, from the will of God for your life.

Rise Up!

When life comes at us hard and places us in an unexpected chokehold, we've got to ground ourselves in those things that are true. "Finally, broth-

Chapter 9: You Don't Have to Do Life Alone

ers and sisters, whatever is true, whatever is noble, whatever is right, whatever is pure, whatever is lovely, whatever is admirable—if anything is excellent or praiseworthy—think about such things" (Philippians 4:8). In order to focus as we should, we need to follow the promptings of the Holy Spirit and listen for the voice of God. The only way we can counterattack the enemy is to spend time in the presence of God. But we must realize that it is difficult to hear God's voice when we are surrounded by distractions.

For a season, I lived a life of utter distraction. I wasted a lot of years going back and forth between focusing on and seeking God, and then switching back to the life I preferred to live. Multitasking is a big one for me. I try to do everything at one time, and I'm not really as productive as I would like to be because I'm not doing anything well. I just do well enough.

Another big distract for a lot of people is the constant consumption of social media. Instagram,

Chapter 9: You Don't Have to Do Life Alone

Snapchat, and Facebook can be a huge problem if not handled with moderation. These things fill your life up with so many insignificant things that you have little to no time to hear from God directly. The lack of focus affects our prayer lives. It is difficult to find time to invest in communicating with God when we are preoccupied with other things.

A lot of us are just zooming through our days so quickly that we have no time set aside to spend with God. I get it. With work, family and all sorts of other obligations, we don't know how we're going to fit it all in. We think we just don't have time to give God a little time, but if we are to stop and think about it, we do. We have time to binge-watch every episode from this season of *Love and Hip Hop*. We try to get a round of texts off during our lunch break. We scroll through Facebook for an hour before bed just to wind down. All this time spent pursuing other things add up to quite a significant chunk of time. Yet, we refuse to unplug and dedicate time to focusing on God.

Chapter 9: You Don't Have to Do Life Alone

Sometimes, we have to pause to seek what God's will is, and we need to unplug for a period of time to seek the voice and will of God. We can no longer afford to coast distractedly through life. The devil is bearing down on us, and he wants to take us out when we least expect it. He wants us to rely on our wits and wisdom, which are unreliable, to keep us shaken and afraid. The enemy knows that we are a hot mess when we don't focus on God, but that's when we are most vulnerable to Satan's tactics.

Earlier in the book, I mentioned that a very direct friend delivered a few words of wisdom that became a turning point in my life. My friend said that the enemy's plan was to keep me consumed with life's challenges and cause me to keep spinning around in circles, chasing my tail. She said that I was equipped for much more than I was attempting to do at the time and that God's purpose for my life was not yet fulfilled. Due to the distractions, I was allowing the devil to delay my journey to a spectacular victory. She encouraged me to get into the Word, spend time speaking with God, and truly believe that on the other side of all my difficulties lay a great destiny.

As I mulled her words over in my mind, I realized that my faith had indeed become buried in the perplexities of life. I had forgotten that "faith is the substance of things hoped for, the evidence of things not seen" (Hebrews 11:1, NKJV). I needed to shift in my thinking and to not dwell on every setback and disappointment I experienced over the years--the shattered dreams and broken heart that were depleting my hopes and energy. God's word had to become the standard to which I improved myself and fortified my resiliency. A steady focus on who He is and who I am in Him was needed. I had to nurture my faith in the unseen and trust God would use the things I was going through to recalibrate my life--on His time--to become the masterpiece He originally intended it to be.

On the Brink of Change

If I could create a step-by-step program for complete change, I would have to base it on the

Chapter 9: You Don't Have to Do Life Alone

verse found in Romans 12:2—"**Do not conform** to the pattern of this world, **but be transformed** by the renewing of your mind. Then you will be able to test and approve what God's will is—his good, pleasing and perfect will" (NIV, emphasis mine). Grieving and disappointment spawn discouragement, depression, stress and many other conditions, all of which begin in the mind and can manifest into physical ailments.

How often have you felt sick to your stomach, sometimes, actually throwing up, because of something you were thinking about? I know when I am stressed and ruminating constantly on something, it takes quite a toll on my body. I have breakouts. I don't walk tall and proud; I'm a little hunched over. I get chronic strep throat. The most perplexing symptom I have of intense stress is when I lay down to go to sleep and it seems as if just moments later, the alarm is going off, signaling for me to wake up. Man! It feels like I haven't gotten a lick of rest at all, and yet, the clock and my remembrance of the time I lay down bears witness that I

Chapter 9: You Don't Have to Do Life Alone

have slept eight hours. It is astounding the way the body responses to stress.

When your mind is afflicting you with memories of traumatic experiences, you can feel debilitated. You become obsessed with what happened, what was said, things you could have said or done, and feelings of shame or regret. Thoughts of how things could have played out differently plague your mind. These thoughts become fantasies that you obsess over — replaying them time and time again in your mind, changing just smidgens of the encounter until your mind becomes tired, brittle and drained.

As humans, we so badly want control of every aspect of our lives. What we wouldn't give for a "do over" pass or a rewind button! We think and overthink until we feel as if we're on the verge of having a major breakdown. We want to stop the madness, but the DVD player of our minds is set on a continuous loop, and we are tied to a chair with our eyes forced open with vice grips, reliving the

Chapter 9: You Don't Have to Do Life Alone

horror, the heartbreak, and the devastation of our circumstances over and over again.

Harassment. Torture. Torment. Our minds are constantly molested by our memories. Just like a predator, memories creep up on us, rendering us helpless as they commit their horrible acts and leave us crumpled by the wayside. As our minds are continually harassed by distressing recollections from our pasts, we become too traumatized and violated to try and maintain any semblance of normalcy. We begin to hide, isolating ourselves from everyone and everything around us.

In the height of my sorrow, all I could do was go to work and function as if I were in some sort of robotic state. I went through the motions, doing what had to be done. After work, I would come home, sit in a chair and just stare into space while the television played unheeded in front of me. I behaved like a person who was shell-shocked.

Chapter 9: You Don't Have to Do Life Alone

One of the things I dreaded most was overcast and rainy days because it seemed the most opportune time for the enemy of my soul, aka my tormentor, to unleash memories and reflections that would haggle at me all day and night. Incidentally, the night — oh, the night would bring a feeling of entrapment like I was confined to a prison. There was no freedom, no peace, and no release. All my pleas to God seemed to drop to the floor. I couldn't seem to get a prayer through. Anytime I spoke to people about what I was feeling, they would ask me if there was anything they could do. Of course, I vehemently said, "Pray!" Maybe they could get a prayer through for me since apparently, God wasn't taking the time to listen to me.

The enemy was working overtime on me. Though I pleaded and begged God to speak to me, give me dreams, have Godly people give me a word from Him or send an angel down to tell me what to do, He was strangely mute. I believed He had abandoned me to flounder about the best I could with no help from Him at all.

Chapter 9: You Don't Have to Do Life Alone

And the devil? I heard him loud and clear. Whenever the enemy spoke, he would lead in with phrases like,

"You know God's ignoring you."

"He doesn't like you."

"You've been so bad all your life. He doesn't want anything to do with you."

"Why do you even try? He's not going to answer you."

Or worst yet, "There can't be a God. If there were truly a "Father" watching out for us, he wouldn't let such awful things happen to people who are just trying to do their best."

As the devil poked and prodded, I became wasted and useless. I listened to him and curled up in the fetal position, almost hoping to expire away.

I was on the brink of doing something drastic. In fact, it was around that time that I told my mom that if something didn't change, I would have to do something drastic. I was drained, and the as-

Chapter 9: You Don't Have to Do Life Alone

saults on my mind and soul were unrelenting. I couldn't take much more. I had had enough!

It was at that point that something shifted. I'm not sure if it was only one thing — my determined declaration to the darkness surrounding my soul that enough was enough or some other imperceptible thing, but I know that things began to change incrementally. During this time of my near breakdown, I began to not just read scriptures and the promises of God, I began to speak them aloud and pray them. I went before the Lord, stubborn as a mule, and basically said, "Look, here. You said this and you said that. What's up with that? Are your words not meant for me? Did you exclude me from your promises?" Though my questions were met with mostly silence, I felt a certain pleasure in being able to let Him know I knew about the promises He'd made and that I was going to hold Him to His word.

It then became a challenge for me. I would read books and scriptures ravenously as if I were

Chapter 9: You Don't Have to Do Life Alone

starving. I guess, in a way, my soul was starving. Even though I was what I considered to be a "good Christian" because I went to church weekly, was involved in various committees and helped different people, I was so busy trying to live a mediocre existence in both life and church that I only gave God's word cursory glances. My worship time in the morning consisted of reading a very short devotional, followed by an equally short prayer, and lasted two to five minutes at the most. My nightly prayers were quick rote prayers with no fervor and very little intensity, and occurred just before I drifted off to sleep. Sometimes, I couldn't even remember praying the night before, and I'd shrug it off saying, "The Lord knows."

My spiritual life was shriveled and emaciated. I did what I had to do because "that's what good Christians do," but I was missing the mark. Just like when I was down and out and just "going through the motions" to make it through work, I was going through the motions to make it through my time with God. I was giving Him the bare minimum. And I was glazing it over with platitudes and appeasements, trying to justify my detachment by asserting to myself that I was doing my best for Him and that I couldn't physically do any better. How repugnant of me to think that the God of the universe should be accepting to only get what was left over from me — the crumbs from my daily life. He had to awaken me to His reality before it was too late. It was time for God to expose me to the fraud I was. It was time for Him to break and remold me into a more useful and beautiful vessel. God allowed the enemy to wreak havoc in what I deemed to be my "perfect" world. I was turned upside down, and I could almost sense the devil dancing a jig of joy at the devastation in my soul.

The Quandary

In life, we are sometimes baffled. We don't know which way to turn, so we throw dice at the wall, hoping God will guide our decisions, but we don't have to hope God is involved in our lives. He gives clear communication and speaks to us directly. We need to adjust our focus and stop to ask God

Chapter 9: You Don't Have to Do Life Alone

what He is trying to say. We must consult God as to what His vision for our lives is. He is trying to communicate with us. We just need to listen.

My near collision with the trucker on the highway would have been an actuality if I had not maintained some semblance of calm and focus on my goal to reach home safely. Many thoughts entered my mind during that frightening time, including, "This is it." Part of me wanted to find a turnoff and head back up the dark highway from where I'd come, but that would have only placed us in greater jeopardy if the trucker decided to turn around behind me in that isolated area. I thought about looking back at him to see what he was doing, but if I'd done this, I wouldn't have been alert if a deer decided to cross the road or if another car appeared in front of me. I had to keep my sights and my mind on what lay ahead. Home. Peace. Security. I didn't have time to be swayed from my path. I gripped the wheel, uttered a prayer and sped on towards my destination. There was a determination that rose up inside of me to keep going.

War Strategies

When we feel defenseless and are subjected to the unscrupulous attacks from our enemy, we can either let them kick us in the knees until we kneel before them, or we can stand and fight through prayer. God doesn't want us meandering through life, bumping our heads and spinning around waywardly in every round-about we come to. He wants to steer us through every distraction and storm that may come our way, but we have to recognize His voice as opposed to that of the enemy.

Whenever you feel led by the promptings that come to your spirit, there are a few strategies you must keep in mind to ensure you are actually hearing from God and not being influenced by the enemy. The following five questions will help you detect if it is God prompting you or not.

1. Is the prompting from God or just your thoughts? Sometimes your own thoughts and feelings can contaminate the message you are receiving. Or, if you are getting the message from others, they may have their

Chapter 9: You Don't Have to Do Life Alone

own agenda. Simply ask God to give you some indication that the words are actually coming from Him. I have found that if they are, there is a feeling of certainty, followed by some sort of confirmation. If it is not from Him, there will be discomfort and uneasiness about it.

2. Is it scriptural? Messages that contradict the word of God are not from God. If it lines up with His word, it is His will.
3. Is it wise? God is never going to suggest you do something stupid. He is a God of order (1 Corinthians 14:33).
4. Does it align with your character? God knows you and would never ask you to do something that He has not equipped you for. He knows how He wired you and for what purposes. He will lead you to where you need to go.
5. What do the Godly people in your life think about it? Ask God to raise up Godly people in your life. Consult those who have a relationship with God on what their opinions

Chapter 9: You Don't Have to Do Life Alone

might be. They may give you the insight you need or, better yet, pray that you receive exactly what you need.

Unleashed!

There are a few pivotal moments in movies that have inspired me so much that they have become a catalyst for change in my life. In the movie *War Room*, Priscilla Shirer's character confronts the devil with a strong declaration that certainly threw him off center.

> I don't know where you are devil, but I know you can hear me…You have played with my mind and had your way long enough. No more! You are done! Jesus is Lord of this house, and that means there's no place for you anymore! So take your lies, your schemes, your accusations, and get out! In Jesus' name! You can't have my marriage, you can't have my daughter, and you sure can't have my man! This house is under

Chapter 9: You Don't Have to Do Life Alone

new management, and that means you are out![1]

That's fire right there! We must remember in the heat of the battle that the enemy will turn tail and run if we meet him head-on with determination, focus directly on our Mighty Warrior, the Lord Himself, and know that when we're in the thick of it, God will never fail us. Just be confident that He is always there to defend and protect you.

Notes

1. Chris Fabry, novelization of War Room (Carol Stream, Il.: Tyndale House, 2015), 163.

Chapter 10
Beauty for Ashes

So you say that you can't go on
Love left you cryin'
And you say all your hope is gone
And what's the use in tryin'?
What you need is to have some faith
Shake off those sad blues
Get yourself a new view
Oh, nothing is as sad as it seems, you know
'Cause someday you'll laugh at the heartache
Someday you'll laugh at the pain
Somehow you'll get through the heartache
Somehow you can get through the rain
When love puts you through the fire
When love puts you through the test
Nothing cures a broken heart

Chapter 10: Beauty for Ashes

Like time, love, and tenderness
When you think your world is over
Baby, just remember this
Nothing heals a broken heart
Like time, love, and tenderness
Time, love, and tenderness
I understand how you're feeling now
And what you've been through
But your world's gonna turn around
So, baby, don't you be blue
All it takes is a little time
To make it better
The hurt won't last forever
Oh, all the tears are gonna dry you know
'Cause someday you'll laugh at the heartache
Someday you'll laugh at the pain
You may be down on your luck
But, baby, that old luck's gonna change
Baby, oh baby you just need some
You just need some
Time, love, and tenderness
Time, love, and tenderness
The hurt ain't gonna last forever

Chapter 10: Beauty for Ashes

Time, love, and tenderness
Time, love, and tenderness[1]

Just like an amputee feels phantom pain after the removal of a limb, a person who has suffered a great and sudden loss of a job, a loved one, or a relationship can face the same type of pain. The feeling that something or someone remains attached to you can be uncanny — especially if they were wrenched away from you in a traumatic way. After the initial shock of a traumatic event and the throes of emotional turmoil you experience along the way, you should reach the point of quiet reflection. The goal at this point is to experience a total and complete release of the pressure that came with the pain of the last few months and embrace an atmosphere of peace and revelation.

The realization, at this point, is that all is actually well. You have survived, and you must move forward to live the best life that you possibly can. You must commit to moving forward. Quit ruminating on what happened. When thoughts come to you, develop a habit of thinking about something positive in the place of that thought. "Consider burning some bridges to your past and to toxic, negative people. Burning may be necessary so you don't go down the same path again.[2]

If someone comes along and wants to dredge up ugly memories, change the subject or quietly give them a blank stare. Trust me — they will begin to feel uncomfortable and quickly start talking about something else. Satan wants to trigger you to remember things that will set you back from full recovery. Resolve to not allow him to keep you stuck in every tar pit you may encounter on your lifelong journey. Quiet your mind so you can glean instruction straight from the throne room of God. He will direct you as to which way to go and what to do from this point forward.

As you survey all the destruction that lies around you, it's easy to throw up your hands and fall into a lifeless heap on the floor. The devil

Chapter 10: Beauty for Ashes

would like nothing better. But God says, "Come to me, all you who are weary and burdened, and I will give you rest. Take my yoke upon you and learn from me, for I am gentle and humble in heart, and you will find rest for your souls. For my yoke is easy and my burden is light" (Matthew 11:28-30). God wants to help you sift through the shards and splinter that are left behind and reconstruct your life into a thing of glory! Just allow Him to guide you where you need to be.

Repairing the Damage

We have suffered terror and pitfalls, ruin and destruction." Lamentations 3:43

It's true. You have gone through some of the worst trials that any human being can go through. You have been subjected to slights and travesties that would stagger the faith of many. You believe that you have been rendered defenseless in a world where evil seems to strike at the very vitality of those who strive to just make sense of life. But God has been with you every step of the way, rallying behind you so that you will get back on your feet. He has done everything in His power to motivate you to press forward. Now, realize the road to recovery will not be easy. The enemy will retaliate and use all he knows about you and your family's propensities to keep you locked up where you are. Satan attacks you so that he can move you further and further away from your destiny, but you must remember you have the whole of heaven at your disposal. God does not leave you to flounder around by yourself. He says, "Do not fear, for I am with you…" (Isaiah 41:10) and "Greater is he that is in me than he that is in the world" (1 John 4:4). Because God is devoted to making sure you succeed and heal from your time of tribulation, you can say with assurance, "I am more than a conqueror through him that loves me" (Romans 8:37).

Road to Restoration

When we just want to get over the pain, we are more prone to rushing the process, but we have got to realize that the process will be smooth on some days, while on other days, it may seem like

Chapter 10: Beauty for Ashes

we are going through a major setback. Commonly, before we achieve complete healing, we go through the grieving process, which is thought to have five separate stages. Those stages are:

- Denial—"This can't be happening to me!"
- Anger—"God, you weren't supposed to let this happen to me!"
- Bargaining—"I'll do anything if I can just have my job back."
- Depression—"I can't take it anymore."
- Acceptance—"I've got to make this work."[3]

As I said before, the enemy will throw you off balance at every stage of the process. Different scenarios will project in your mind that will play on your emotions and bring you unrealistic expectations of how things could possibly turn out. Or fear may set in which causes you to doubt that things will ever get back to what you grew to know as "normal." The strategy is to make you hesitant in your resolve to gain ground and trip up your momentum. This is when you have to purposely focus on God's goodness and mercy. You can be assured of this: He hasn't deserted you (…lo, I am with you always, even unto the end of the world. *Matthew 28:20*).

It's Alive!
> *The hand of the Lord was on me, and he brought me out by the Spirit of the Lord and set me in the middle of a valley; it was full of bones. He led me back and forth among them, and I saw a great many bones on the floor of the valley, bones that were very dry. He asked me, "Son of man, can these bones live?"*
> *I said, "Sovereign Lord, you alone know."*
> *Then he said to me, "Prophesy to these bones and say to them, 'Dry bones, hear the word of the Lord! This is what the Sovereign Lord says to these bones: I will make breath enter you, and you will come to life.*

Chapter 10: Beauty for Ashes

I will attach tendons to you and make flesh come upon you and cover you with skin; I will put breath in you, and you will come to life. Then you will know that I am the Lord.'"
So I prophesied as I was commanded. And as I was prophesying, there was a noise, a rattling sound, and the bones came together, bone to bone. 8 I looked, and tendons and flesh appeared on them and skin covered them, but there was no breath in them.
Then he said to me, "Prophesy to the breath; prophesy, son of man, and say to it, 'This is what the Sovereign Lord says: Come, breath, from the four winds and breathe into these slain, that they may live.'" So I prophesied as he commanded me, and breath entered them; they came to life and stood up on their feet—a vast army.

Chapter 10: Beauty for Ashes

Then he said to me: "Son of man, these bones are the people of Israel. They say, 'Our bones are dried up and our hope is gone; we are cut off.' Therefore prophesy and say to them: 'This is what the Sovereign Lord says: My people, I am going to open your graves and bring you up from them; I will bring you back to the land of Israel. Then you, my people, will know that I am the Lord, when I open your graves and bring you up from them. I will put my Spirit in you and you will live, and I will settle you in your own land. Then you will know that I the Lord have spoken, and I have done it, declares the Lord.'" (Ezekiel 37:1-14)

Unlike Frankenstein's Monster, when God brings together dehydrated parts to form a living, breathing human, it is not some grotesque

Chapter 10: Beauty for Ashes

amalgamation that runs amok throughout the land, wreaking havoc. As He sifts through the rubble of your life, nothing is wasted. Your past, though it may not look so good at first glance, upon closer inspection, can yield some usable fragments that will bring wisdom to, not only you but to whomever God places in your path thereafter that needs to hear your story.

Right now, you may be looking at a pile of dry bones. Dead. Nothing to do with them but bury them. The love of your life is gone. You'll never love again. The job that you reported to faithfully for the past 12 years has gone to someone else. Your children don't seem to have time for you in their lives anymore. Your dreams of owning a business and traveling the world have been replaced by the nightmare of debt.

You think the time has expired for you to have the life your heart was set on having. "It's okay," you say, trying to convince yourself. You push your desires to the back burner, yet your heart

Chapter 10: Beauty for Ashes

thumps faster when the longings reappear. You shake your head and try to refocus your thoughts on the safe things in your life — things that don't require you to step out and possibly get your feelings hurt once again.

God will not allow your dry bones to remain in this barren wasteland of dashed dreams and reneged promises. He helps you blow the dust off your disappointments, and He'll speak to you about the condition of those bones. He will tell you how they came to be that way in the first place. He'll reveal what devices were used to assail them and bring about their demise. He will not let them lie in repose for long. He will breathe life back into them and show you the beautiful potential — the potential He had planned since the foundation of the world for those bones. He restores the bones to life, and all He asks is that this new life is dedicated to Him.

God originally intended that we would commit our lives to His sovereign will. After all,

Chapter 10: Beauty for Ashes

He created us, knit us in our mothers' wombs, and knows how many hairs we have on our heads at any given time. He wanted to provide you with the wisdom to make the right decisions for your life and shelter you under His shadow so that you can perform His will. But sometimes, in the course of our lives, we place the diamond that He is aside while we chase after glitter. We create idols for ourselves of the things and people that wander into our lives. We take our attention away from Him and don't consult Him, the Almighty God, about any aspect of our lives. We go ahead and place ourselves in situations that were never part of His plan for us. Yet, God's intent on giving us freedom of choice does not sabotage what we have set into motion. He allows it to play out, patiently waiting for us to come full circle back to Him.

When things happen contrary to our wishes, God allows them to come to a head, and then He steps in. He brings us, in our pain, back around full circle, revealing who He is and His desires for us. He shows us that He is Alpha and Omega — He is

Chapter 10: Beauty for Ashes

there for us at the beginning of all things, and He is there for us to run to when things turn bad. He will strengthen, soothe and help us rest and hear His voice. Just like the stanzas of the song at the beginning of the chapter, your perspective will change with time and the love and tenderness of God. When it's over, we will be made whole again.

Notes

1. *Bolton, M. & Warren, D. (1991). Time, Love, and Tenderness. Retrieved from https://genious.com/Michael-bolton-time-love-and-tenderness-lyrics*
2. *Stewart, Melanie (Butterfly Beauty). 7/20/15, 7:17 PM. Tweet.*
3. *Five Stages of Grief by Elisabeth Kubler Ross & David Kessler. (n.d.). Retrieved December 12, 2017, from https://grief.com/the-five-stages-of-grief/*

Chapter 11
The Struggle

Life has many ways of testing a person's will, either by having nothing happen at all or by having everything happen all at once.—Paulo Coelho

One December night in 2012, a friend called and asked me if I'd heard about a promising young linebacker named Jovan Belcher, who'd just shot his girlfriend and then committed suicide in front of his coach and others. I had not heard about it. I had stopped watching the news because it never informed more than it made me anxious. The only time I learned about something going on in the world was through word-of-mouth or Facebook updates. I was curious to find out what compelled this man to commit such a horrendous act, so I did some

Chapter 11: The Struggle

research. I found that Belcher became jealous when his 22-year old girlfriend and mother of his three-month-old daughter attended a concert with a few friends. He became suspicious when she arrived home later than expected and thought she may be attracted to the artist who'd performed. Added to this was the fact that they'd both been experiencing extreme strain in their relationship due to his demanding schedule and the new baby. Coupled with his apparent insecurity, the perfect foreshadowing of the catastrophic event was born and Mr. Belcher reacted to it. Now, a child sits motherless and fatherless in the aftermath.

God reveals in His word that in the last days…

> *…difficult times will come. For men will be lovers of self, lovers of money, boastful, arrogant, revilers, disobedient to parents, ungrateful, unholy, unloving, irreconcilable, malicious gossips, without self-control, brutal, haters of good,*

Chapter 11: The Struggle

treacherous, reckless, conceited, lovers of pleasure rather than lovers of God, holding to a form of godliness, although they have denied its power; Avoid such men as these. For among them are those who enter into households and captivate weak women weighed down with sins, led on by various impulses, always learning and never able to come to the knowledge of the truth. (2 Timothy 3:1-7- NASB)

There is a dark and ominous cloud on the horizon. Insecurity, jealousy, and just plain ole selfishness have become pandemics in our society. These three things lead to all manner of inappropriate behaviors. Disconnecting, unconcern, discourteousness, lying, stealing, vengeance, domination, and abuse — it is a certainty that all of the seven deadly sins are also interwoven with these.

Chapter 11: The Struggle

As people become more and more concerned with only themselves, they are more apt to do what they feel they have to do, or become resigned to taking their "last resorts" out of desperation. There's a sort of desperation that paves the steps of selfish and insecure people, and desperate people do desperate things. They feel they are accountable to no one other than themselves, and no matter what the repercussions may be, they are going to have their way by any means necessary. They couldn't care less about you, what you might think or what will happen to you. And because of their shallow relationship with God — if they even know Him at all — they have no internal barometer, like their conscience, with which to gauge their actions.

Well, What to Do?

You must realize that the moral decline of the world is not a weight that you need to place on your shoulders. The Lord is taking care of business, so don't worry. Do what you can by being a true representative of the love and character of God, but

Chapter 11: The Struggle

don't overwhelm yourself by trying to take everything upon yourself and agonizing over every report of bad news that comes your way. The truth of the matter is that you must become completely in tune with God and communicate with Him constantly. This is the main tool for survival on Earth.

There's a bulletin board at my school that says "READ like a wolf eats." One may ask how exactly a wolf eats. Ravenously. Insatiably. Voraciously. The same action should be taken in our relationship with God. We should hunger for Him and long to spend time with Him. We should talk with Him about everything. Non-stop. No one understands you better. No one loves you more than the one who suffered and died for you. As you talk with God, don't get wrapped up in your own soliloquy. This is not a one-man or one-woman show. God is your Director, Producer, and fellow Cast Member. He's in it with you, and just as two actors have an exchange of dialogue on stage, we should have a two-way conversation with God.

Chapter 11: The Struggle

Psalm 46:10 (NIV) reads, *"He says, 'Be still, and know that I am God; I will be exalted among the nations; I will be exalted in the earth.'"* Stillness is imperative for a close relationship with your Creator. He wants to hear from you, and then, He wants you to quietly wait for His response. And there is no telling how He will respond. It might be through something someone says to you just perchance. It might be through His word or through your reading. It might be through some event or special circumstance. It might be through a still, small voice. Just be prayerfully attentive to any and every modus God uses. God has foreseen and prepared for every contingency. You have no reason to fear. Every snare of the enemy has been uncovered and lay bare before God, and every planned attack has been thwarted and counterattacked. All you need to do is trust Him to take care of you. Just keep reminding yourself that God is with you, He will never forsake you and you can depend on Him.

The only thing that can truly produce a change in us and our circumstances is an intimate

Chapter 11: The Struggle

relationship with God. You can't intimately know someone if you don't communicate with them, spend time with them, and learn all about them. With God, this is not complicated —talk to God and listen. Talk and listen. After this, take what you hear and live it. And include Him in everything you do, after all, *"Apart from [God] you can do **nothing**"* (John 15:5 NIV, emphasis mine).

Chapter 12
Get Out

In 2017, a comedian named Jordan Peele debuted as director of a dark, psychological thriller/social commentary, entitled *Get Out*! The film introduces the viewer to the story of a young, interracial couple, comprised of a talented African-American photographer named Chris and his alluring, college student girlfriend, Rose. As the movie opens, Chris and Rose are traveling to spend the weekend at Rose's family home so that Chris can meet the parents. When they arrive, the family seems welcoming enough, but Chris senses something that is unsettling just beneath the surface.

There are very few African-Americans in the area, and those whom Chris does meet display

Chapter 12: Get Out

some very bizarre behaviors. At a party the family is throwing to introduce him to the community, Chris is introduced to a black man whom he covertly takes a picture of. But the flash from his phone's camera seems to agitate the man, and he begins to approach Chris in a hostile manner, screaming in his face, "Get out!" The man has to be restrained by those near him as he continues to scream at Chris. Later, through some investigation of the photo by his friend back home, Chris finds out that the freakish occurrences at his girlfriend's parents' home concealed a more sinister fate for him if he, indeed, does not "get out." Often, directors like Mr. Peele, who create thrillers and horror movies, insert a scene where the unwitting victims are told by a neighbor or a disembodied voice to "get out" of wherever they are at the moment. Usually, the plot of the movie revolves around the fact that the individual does not heed the warning, often with dire consequences. But every warning in every movie is not to be considered a threat. There are times that someone tells a person to get out, not to scare them, but as advice that they should not

Chapter 12: Get Out

remain stagnant — that they should move forward.

There are times our all-wise, and all-knowing God admonishes us to break away from that which has become all too familiar in order to reach our destinies. He encourages us to escape the ordinary to acquaint ourselves with the extraordinary.

Escape

While some people need little motivation to remove themselves from a situation that is hindering them from living the best life possible, there are those of us who have to be spurred on by direct nudges from the elbow of God Himself. We shuffle through life full of trepidation and fear, vacillating in an atmosphere of resignation — resignation to a life of commonness — a life that's not thriving — a life wasted in apathy and boredom. But God wants us to make progress. He wants to transform our run-of-the-mill, middle-of-the-road existences into amazingly wonderful lives where every possibility is open to us.

Chapter 12: Get Out

In spite of how our trials seem to manifest, there are gifts, promises, and things God has deposited in you that He wants to manifest into reality. Right now. The dreams you have that have been lying dormant inside of you to make a difference, start that business, or live a happy, peaceful life are now activated by the power of God's word. As you draw closer to Him and take your rightful place as His child, you become a joint heir to all the power, miracles, and promises heaven can bestow. The dreams you have buried deep inside you can be resurrected if you only press forward and pursue the will of God.

God has a purpose for our lives, but we need to escape the mindsets, the complacency, and the hindrances to embrace this purpose. We must get out of where we are and experience the fullness of life with God because sometimes, we can't reach the full extent of our blessings where we are.

> *Terah took his son Abram, his grandson Lot son of Haran, and his daughter-in-law Sarai, the wife of*

Chapter 12: Get Out

his son Abram, and together they set out from Ur of the Chaldeans to go to Canaan. But when they came to Harran, they settled there.
Terah lived 205 years, and he died in Harran. -- Genesis 11:31, 32

The Lord had said to Abram, "Go from your country, your people and your father's household to the land I will show you.
"I will make you into a great nation, and I will bless you; I will make your name great, and you will be a blessing. I will bless those who bless you, and whoever curses you I will curse; and all peoples on earth will be blessed through you."
So Abram went, as the Lord had told him; and Lot went with him. Abram was seventy-five years old when he set out from Harran. --Genesis 12:1-4

Chapter 12: Get Out

Abram had a call on his life. A call for greatness. God had countless blessings He wanted to give Abram and his family, but first, he needed to get away from where he was. God told Abram that He was calling him to greatness, but first, there were some things Abram needed to do. If he was to, indeed, be the father of a great nation, he had to leave his country and kindred, and leave his father's household. Abram was raised in a place called Ur. He and his family left Ur and ended up in a place called Harran, which means "parched"[1] and he settled there. He settled in a dry place — a place with little to no life and with no improvement in sight. Abram and his family settled in a place that God never intended for them to settle in. God told him to get out of that dusty, dried up area. God's intention was not for him to settle. The same goes for us — we tend to settle; we settle for unsatisfactory relationships — we settle for unfulfilling careers — we settle for not reaching our potential. But God is saying to us, "No, I'm calling you to greatness. Don't settle in that parched place."

Chapter 12: Get Out

To get Abram out of the settled mindset, the first thing He asked him to do was to change his location. God is telling us to change our locations, after all, we will never come into our greatness if we remain where we are. For Abram, God was focused on his geographical location or where he was positioned at the time. He needed to relocate to receive the blessings God had for him. Sometimes, we need to change where we are in order to be blessed. Think of Will Smith in the 90's television show *Fresh Prince of Bel-Air*. For the theme song of the show, Will raps a little bit about the circumstances that caused him to have to transition from Philadelphia to Bel-Air.

> *Now this is the story all about how*
> *My life got flipped, turned upside down*
> *And I'd like to take a minute, just sit right there, I'll tell you how*
> *I became the prince of a town called Bel-Air."*
> *In west Philadelphia born and raised*
> *On the playground was where I spent most*

Chapter 12: Get Out

> *of my days*
> *Chillin' out maxin' relaxin' all cool*
> *And all shooting some b-ball outside of the school*
> *When a couple of guys who were up to no good*
> *Started making trouble in my neighborhood*
> *I got in one little fight, and my mom got scared*
> *She said, "You're movin' with your auntie and uncle in Bel-Air."* [2]

Will's mother understood that there were elements in his community that were keeping him from becoming the great man that God had called him to be. He had become a target for the miscreants of society, and they would not leave him alone if he stayed in the same environment they were in. For this reason, his mother made sure he wasn't under their radar by changing his whereabouts in the world.

Rerouting

Some of us also have to make a drastic move if we want to come into greatness — whether that move is physical, by changing where we are geographically, or whether the move is mental, by changing where we are spiritually. I realized that if I were to ever reach the future God had planned for me, I would not remain where I was spiritually. It soon became clear that it was time to take life to another level. Not only did I need to change spiritually, but I needed to make a big mental shift because at times, I would find myself stuck in a mindset full of negativity and stinking thinking. It was through the guidance of the Holy Spirit that I made the shift from glum to joyful. God would have held off on giving me the talents and skills I needed to fulfill my destiny if I hadn't moved when He told me to move. I would have languished as a mere shadow of what I was meant to be. God may not need you to move geographically, spiritually, or mentally. Sometimes, He needs you to move forward emotionally. The emotional issues and soul wounds need to be taken care of before you can go to the next level. Maybe He needs to move you to a better financial footing. Living check-to-check and above your means is not how God wants you to live. The bottom line is, God says He has identified the purpose, potential, and possibilities that lie within you. You are pregnant with all the hopes and dreams that He has anointed you with. There are some of you who are one step away from coming into your purpose, and all you have to do is reroute.

They Are Not For You

Not only did He say to change your location, He said that many of you need to get away from some of your kinfolk. God is telling you to get away from those people who will hold you back — people who don't believe you have anything special about you. Or, if they do believe, they don't want you to look better than they do. God knows you can't come into the greatness He has for you if you continue to surround yourself with those who don't have your vision. They will limit you and essentially limit your ability to influence others for the Kingdom. Don't allow them to hold you back.

Chapter 12: Get Out

Recognize that not everyone can go where you're going because not everyone will be able to see what you see. Not everyone will be able to see the power of God in your life. There are people in your life who can't see your heart and understand why you are the way you are. They don't have your vision because God never gave it to them in the first place. He gave it to you. Your connection with certain people will impede your progress.

Pastor Ron Carpenter, Jr., in his book *Necessity of an Enemy*, states that even Jesus had to keep his inner circle small.[3] Even though He had twelve disciples that were very close to Him, whenever He needed closer companionship, He always chose The Big Three — Peter, James, and John. Jesus understood that everyone couldn't go where He was going — they would only hinder him. So, there are some friendships that you're going to have to let go of. There are some people who you've got to let go of before you reach your next level.

Chapter 12: Get Out

Break Away

Sometimes, you have got to get out of your family home. God told Abram to leave his father's household because, as a Chaldean, Abram's father, Terah, most likely worshiped the idols of his people. Abram could not serve God and reside in a home where he was surrounded by idols and the worship of false gods. He needed to leave all that behind so that he could be led by God without distraction. God needs you to break away from some of the customs and habits that are common among your people. Maybe alcoholism is prevalent in your family. Maybe your environment was abusive. Perhaps, some things happened in your household that served to humiliate and degrade you. The enemy tries to hurt you in the place you should feel most secure. He wants to kill your potential at inception. We see this in the Bible. When Moses was a baby, Pharaoh wanted all male children killed or thrown in the Nile. When Jesus was a child, Herod decreed that all boys three years of age and under be killed. Why? Because the enemy tries to terminate our potential while we're young. If he

Chapter 12: Get Out

can't get you in the womb or soon after, the devil will subject you to negativity throughout your developmental years. This negativity is designed to keep you tethered to your past and keep you from coming into your greatness as you grow older.

Once You Know This

God is going to call you to greatness, but you've got to get out. Get out from among your family. Get out of your limiting mindsets. Get out of where you are at this moment. You are full of greatness. Affirm yourself. Ignite a fire under your lethargy and fear. Realize that you are awesome. Understand that you have great possibilities and a wonderful destiny that lies before you. Remember 1 Corinthians 2:9—*"But as it is written, Eye hath not seen, nor ear heard, neither have entered into the heart of man, the things which God hath prepared for them that love him."* God has some amazing surprises for your future, and He has equipped you with everything you need to be a success in this world. All you have to do is **Get Out**.

Notes

1. *Ebccnj.org. (2018). They came to Haran. [online] Available at: http://www.ebccnj.org/chn/wyt20050619tx-t.htm [Accessed 12 December 2017].*
2. *Genius. (2017). DJ Jazzy Jeff & the Fresh Prince – Fresh Prince of Bel-Air. [online] Available at: https://genius.com/Dj-jazzy-jef-f-and-the-fresh-prince-fresh-prince-of-bel-air-lyrics [Accessed 12 Dec. 2017].*

Chapter 13

The End of the Journey (Or Is It?)

Hey, heard you were up all night
Thinking about how your world ain't right
And you wonder if things will ever get better
And you're asking why is it always raining on you
When all you want is just a little good news
Instead of standing there stuck out in the weather

Oh, don't hang your head
It's gonna end
God's right there
Even if it's hard to see Him
I promise you that He still cares

When the waves are taking you under
Hold on just a little bit longer
He knows that this is gonna make you stronger,

Chapter 13: The End of the Journey (Or Is It?)

stronger
The pain ain't gonna last forever
And things can only get better
Believe me
This is gonna make you stronger
Gonna make you stronger, stronger, stronger
Believe me, this is gonna make you Stronger

Try and do the best you can
Hold on and let Him hold your hand
And go on and fall into the arms of Jesus
Oh, lift your head it's gonna end
God's right there
Even when you just can't feel Him
I promise you that He still cares

'Cause if He started this work in your life
He will be faithful to complete it
If only you believe it
He knows how much it hurts
And I'm sure that He's gonna help you get through this

Chapter 13: The End of the Journey (Or Is It?)

When the waves are taking you under
Hold on just a little bit longer
He knows that this is gonna make you stronger,
stronger
The pain ain't gonna last forever
In time it's gonna get better
Believe me
This is gonna make you stronger.[1]

This journey has been one wrought with many tears and heartfelt pleadings, humility, and utter surrender. Nevertheless, I have learned this one thing about the Lord — He is not the elusive spirit of my nightmares who deems me unworthy of receiving even the most minuscule of blessings. I've been blaming Him for everything when all the time, I should have been blaming the enemy and his deceitful, conniving ways.

One point of faith that I have grasped upon is that God does not want us to live life with uncertainty and confusion. He knows that our human instincts make us want to know everything

Chapter 13: The End of the Journey (Or Is It?)

from the beginning to the end. This is so we can influence and control the outcome. Such pursuits lead to doubt and frustration when things don't flow as we believe they should. These traits are marks of the enemy brought forth to plant doubt and faithlessness in our hearts. The enemy makes God seem like some intricate puzzle to decode — some labyrinth to plod and stumble our way through, but through this journey, I have discovered that God is not like that at all. As Jesus says, *"My yoke is easy..."* (Matthew 11:30).

There is nothing complex or confusing about our Father's love. He wants the best for us, and He does not want to trick and laugh at us as we go through our quandaries. You wouldn't believe how many times I've heard that God has a "sense of humor" — that He places us in these trials to make us feel like mice in the maze, just for His entertainment. He loves us. God equals Love, as the scripture (1 John 4:8) says so succinctly. He pursues us. He does everything in His power to make us come to Him directly — to reason with Him — to tell

Chapter 13: The End of the Journey (Or Is It?)

Him how we feel — to share our hopes, dreams, and disappointments with Him. He will then take the time to show us whose we are — that we are a royal priesthood, a chosen generation. He wants to show us that anything we desire that fits into His will for our lives will be granted to us — that He will doubly increase us for the time and torment of the "locusts" that have devastated our lives — that He is watching over us and His ultimate desire is to have us at home with Him. He is a God who is interested in the concerns of our hearts, and He does not look smugly upon our troubles.

The conditions we are in and the experiences we go through are all brought on by us allowing ourselves to get all wrapped in the enemy's emotional entanglements. This causes us to lose sight of our potential goals and gives us a false view of what God is doing on our behalf. It causes us to blame and dishonor Him. We have got to realize that all negativity and strife comes from the enemy. His main goal is to prove to the universe that God's great plan and the people whom He chose to save with it are all failed experiments. He wants us to believe that we (humans) are not capable of withstanding great amounts of pain, either physical or mental, without shaking their fists at the sky and distrusting their maker. He seeks to assault us and point his finger at God all the while he is doing all he can to trip us up. His goal is to distract us from his beastly ways while we look up to God in frustration. We waste time blaming our Father while our enemy is distracting us with minutiae.

More Than a Conqueror

The five months Russ grappled with the pain of a misdiagnosed injury were the most excruciating of his life. He was initially led to believe that his injury was merely a pulled muscle and was not as severe as he thought. Medical professionals, friends, and family members told him that it was all in his mind — that the pain was just the result of an over-stressed mind. Yet, for Russ, it didn't matter how many people told him he was healthy, he instinctively knew that what he was feeling was real.

Chapter 13: The End of the Journey (Or Is It?)

He wasn't satisfied until he found someone to support him in what he believed to be real.

Russ always berated himself for his low tolerance for pain, yet for some reason, this new painful experience brought more than an irritation to the area. This pain brought with it doubt that he would ever get better and intense anxiety that he would no longer perform well at work or in his personal life. When he came to me agonizing about how he felt his life had ended and how demoralized he felt due to the pain, I immediately told him to snap out of it. After all, there were people who we both knew that were going through much more traumatic pain, like stage four cancer. Even though they were obviously suffering, they carried on with few complaints. Did he actually think a pulled muscle that would eventually heal could rival their pain? "Come on, man. Be logical," I said with barely concealed annoyance in my voice. Russ skulked away, disappointed at my lack of empathy.

Chapter 13: The End of the Journey (Or Is It?)

One night, while he was at work, fear gripped his heart so greatly that he had a panic attack. While he sat at his desk shaking and sweating, he cried out to God. Even though the pain was dissipating due to time and treatment, Russ feared it would reappear and prevent him from concentrating at work or continuing with the activities that he enjoyed. He felt paralyzed by the fear that gripped his heart with newfound vigor. As he sat hyperventilating, he felt he'd heard the voice of God speaking directly to him, and what he heard changed the trajectory of his thinking. God spoke directly to Russ's heart, telling him that everything — every pain, every disappointment — in his life happened to prepare him for situations he would experience later on in life. It was all to strengthen his character. When those difficult times came, Russ realized his job was to stay in position with God. The more attacks he received, the closer he needed to draw to God. And as he drew closer, Russ began developing the power of influence — the power to influence others to seek the will and the ways of God.

Chapter 13: The End of the Journey (Or Is It?)

Russ soon came to realize that as he activated the power of influence, he could easily see how the enemy was operating his life. He began to brush away the strife that had become all too common to his everyday life like dust. He realized that the power of God's influence upon him gave him access to all the power of the Kingdom. Russ's healing began as he relinquished control of his life to the God of the universe who controls his destiny. The place where he used to subject God to accusations and blame, he now brought assurance and trust. He saw how the enemy distracted him from all the good in his life and caused him to focus on that which stifled him. He came to realize that no matter how it looked, God was actually moving through his life, sorting things and placing them in order.

Russ's desire to draw closer to his one true Help grew and he began to offer Him heartfelt worship, instead of fear and complaining. Russ slowly walked out of his spiritual exile by reminding himself of who God is and what He has done for him over the course of his life. He allowed God, rather

Chapter 13: The End of the Journey (Or Is It?)

than Satan, to penetrate his mind with words of hope and peace. Eventually, he became transformed into a person who influences others to totally trust in God. As a result, his antagonism lost its power and fell by the wayside. The pain Russ experienced in his life developed within him a certain strength that has been a catalyst in encouraging others to seek the One who has helped him change so drastically. His life has become a shining beacon for those who long for substance. It only took him a little time to understand that God was not his enemy and his pain was not the end. And in learning this lesson, Russ became aware that he had all the power of God's kingdom at his disposal.

Reclaiming My Time

My friends tell me that I have hidden the pain so well that they truly believed there was nothing wrong, but in my soul, I know that I still have so much more healing to do. It's funny — when I think I have reached the end of my traumatized feelings, they soon reappear with a vengeance. I awaken in the middle of the night with sorrow weighing

Chapter 13: The End of the Journey (Or Is It?)

heavily on me and I begin praying fervently for peace to come to me — for God to lift me in His soothing embrace. There have been nights when I've prayed all night long with no indication of any hope. I've cried out for mercy with such vehemence that I feel as if I can't cry anymore, but it's not long before my eyes well up again.

When life throws circumstances at you that leave you feeling empty, tired and drained, it is so easy to feel like giving up and throwing in the towel.

"What am I doing all this for?"
"What good is it anyway?" I'm not going to get better!"

Like Job's wife, you think, "What's the use? Just curse God and die!" Many people give up totally at this point — filled with such despair that they wallow in their hopelessness and squander their lives away, giving it to sadness and misery. And they do die — either spiritually or physically.

Chapter 13: The End of the Journey (Or Is It?)

Now, I can't pretend that I have relished every aspect of this journey. But one thing has been obvious — it was a little hazy at first, but as I stumbled forward, it became clearer — that there has been an unseen presence, a guide who has led me to places I've never dreamed I would be. This Guide has set me in places where my heart has been set free, where I feel so connected to the One who loves me like no other — the One who sees me for who I really am and who still loves me unconditionally — the One who I can run to broken and battered, and feel His loving and warm embrace and his whispered assurances that everything will be alright.

It is so easy for us, as humans, to put our trust and hope in things that leave us feeling abandoned and empty. We pursue careers, people, and opportunities that seem like they will be the next big thing to fill our lives and bring meaning to this journey that we call life. Yet, nothing satisfies. There is still a searching, a longing, and an empty

Chapter 13: The End of the Journey (Or Is It?)

space in our souls, and we keep struggling to find that one thing that will quench our thirst.

A Familiar Story

She went to get water at the well in the center of town. It was part of her routine — to travel with a few containers in her hand and gather water for her household. After all, she had dishes to wash, food to cook, and a thirsty man at home. When she arrived at the well, she was surprised to find a Jewish man there who looked weary and thirsty. But there was something underneath the surface that seemed different about this man — something inexplicable. That's when He spoke. "Oh, He must be crazy — that must be the difference," she thought to herself. Didn't this man, who was obviously a Jew, know that Jews did not speak to their despised enemies, the Samaritans? And didn't He know that, as a Samaritan woman, she was definitely abhorred by His kind? What's that?! He's asking for water? Surely, He knows anything she touches and gives Him would be contaminated. She had to put a stop to this craziness before something bad happened.

Chapter 13: The End of the Journey (Or Is It?)

She said, "Sir, don't you realize that I am a Samaritan woman? And you still want a drink of water?" The man did not hesitate but told her, in no uncertain terms, that if she knew who He was, she would have asked Him if He could have drawn the water for her. She stared at Him, bemused. He had no bucket or container of any kind that she could see. How in the world would He have gotten the water out of the well?

Then, the man went on to tell her that the water He offered did not quench thirst temporarily like the water before them, but would quench the thirst for all time. Her eyes lit up — to never have to walk again to this well and lug heavy containers of waters back home appealed to her. "Where can I get some of this water?" she asked eagerly. He told her to go get her husband, to which she answered that she did not have one. The man shocked her by revealing that the man she was currently living with was indeed, not her husband, and she had had five others before him. "What manner of witchcraft was this? How does He know that about me?" she

Chapter 13: The End of the Journey (Or Is It?)

thought. Did He know she was trying to find true satisfaction — a home for her heart? Was He aware that her experiences with all the men in her life had left her with a desire to call it quits and run until she couldn't run anymore? Did He know that she'd just recently resigned herself to living a life of hopelessness?

Just like that woman, our souls cry out to God without us even realizing it. We thirst for His touch. Our hearts are hungry and longing for His unfailing love. Yet, desperately, we grasp after every wind of doctrine, seeking something intangible to fulfill our needs. We call out with all our hearts, not sure of what we need, but instinctively knowing it's out there somewhere. As we travel down the road of confusion, as darkness surrounds us and chaos closes in, we fall to our knees before the One who is our only hope. That's when He picks up and shows us that beyond our struggles, beyond the storm clouds that seem to suffocate our minds, there is the sun (Son) waiting to shine into our lives, revealing the shadows that are in our souls and van-

Chapter 13: The End of the Journey (Or Is It?)

quishing them to the nether regions of space. He shows us the truth of what He is about and who we are. He shows us the empty places within our souls and shines a light in the darkened corners where our heartaches, fears, and shame hide. And though He does not reveal everything about the many questions we have, He plants in us a desire and a passion to press forward towards the outstanding destinies He has for us. He promised that everything will work out for our good, and even though we may have to be patient and wait, He makes the wait worthwhile by restoring and helping us surpass what we have lost.

The Best Part of the Story Thus far

I have begun approaching God with the mindset that He is not trying to perplex me with some great mental challenge to confuse me with before He gives me the prize in which I seek. God just wants to have me come to Him and tell Him in the simplest way possible what I am seeking. The same goes for you. Approach God with everything that is in your heart, come reason with Him and take

Chapter 13: The End of the Journey (Or Is It?)

the time to listen and get to know His heart and will through meditating on His word. He is a great and loving Friend. Any question that is on your mind will be answered by God. He will not allow you to grapple with turmoil without placing the right people, the best opportunities, the most effective words, the powerful visions, prayers, hopes and environments in your life. God sees all, He knows all, and He can certainly handle all. Hold on, be strong, and trust His guidance.

Notes

1. *Glover, B., Stevenson, C., & Garcia, D.A. (2011). Stronger. Retrieved from https://genius.com/Mandisa-stronger-lyrics*

www.ingramcontent.com/pod-product-compliance
Lightning Source LLC
LaVergne TN
LVHW051554070426
835507LV00021B/2583